The Happiness Code

Richmond Shee

Scripture quotations are from the King James Authorized Version.

ISBN-13: 978-069298731-5

Purple
dreamer
Publishers

With gratitude to the Lord Jesus Christ for the gifts of eternal life and wisdom, and to my beloved wife, Jody.

Table of Contents

1 – Level Set

H as life left you sad, empty, and in despair? You just can't seem to find happiness no matter what you do? In frustration, you yell out, "Hello happiness! Where are you? Why are you so elusive?"

Riches say, "I feel your pain, but it's not in me." Knowledge says, "It's not with me." Pleasure, power, and possessions say, "We haven't seen it." Success says, "I've only heard about it."

Search no more, **"The Happiness Code"** shows how to live a meaningful life that matters, taking you on a journey into the Bible book of Ecclesiastes to reveal the vanities under the sun and the path of true happiness as set by the Creator God.

The truths and wisdom in Ecclesiastes are of God and were penned by Solomon, who also wrote the books of Proverbs and The Song of Solomon. You have access to the mind of God as well as the learned lessons and advice from Solomon, the wisest and richest man who ever lived. You will be able to:

- Recognize vanities and not waste your life chasing after meaningless and inconsequential things. In the first 11 chapters, you will understand why the things you do for happiness don't work.

- Live a joyful life that counts for the cause of Christ by practicing the wisdom in chapters 12 thru 16 and the recommendations throughout this book.

- Learn the book of Ecclesiastes and use **"The Happiness Code"** as a reference commentary. As a young person, I was attracted to wisdom literature, even though I didn't understand much of it. I remember making multiple attempts at understanding and applying "The Art of War" by Sun Tzu and finally gave up. When I became a Christian, I spent a lot of time in the books of Proverbs and Ecclesiastes. Most of the sayings, knowledge, and principles were over my head. But now, after more than 20 years of walking with the Lord and experiencing how wisdom works, I hope to explain the book of Ecclesiastes to you. My Asian background and upbringing turn out to be helpful, because some of the statements and examples in the book of Ecclesiastes make perfect sense to Asians, but not so much to Westerners.

Readers who will benefit the most from this book are Christians who love God, love His word, and are seeking a happy and fulfilled life.

Everyone who comes into this world is predisposed to seeking happiness *"under the sun,"* a phrase that is repeated 27 times in the book of Ecclesiastes, or 30 times counting the phrases *"under the heaven"* and *"under heaven."* Why such a focus on the world? God wants you to know what you can expect under the sun, including what happens if you set your affections on the things of the world. The lateral picture is not pretty, and for this reason many people find the book of Ecclesiastes depressing. This is because the book shows that there is no happiness and satisfaction under the sun, no matter what people do. The notion that this world has something to make a person happy is a mirage. Failure to recognize this results in misery and unhappiness.

The world is doing a fine job at making people's lives meaningless and miserable by brain washing them into thinking that it can give them everything they desire, including happiness, health, and wealth. They can have, do, or be anything they want. They are the center of focus. The world entices them with everything imaginable to captivate and keep them from experiencing true happiness.

To experience true happiness, you must break free from the world's gravitational pull on your affections and go above the sun, where God is. *Colossians 3:1 If ye then be risen with Christ, seek those things which are above, where Christ sitteth on the right hand of God. (2) Set your affection on things above, not on things on the earth.*

The code of happiness dictates that you must accept Jesus Christ as both Lord and Savior and set your affections on heavenly things. You may disagree. The way to settle this is for you to try everything the world has to offer like Solomon did. If you still come up empty, I invite you to try the Bible's way. By this time, what do you have to lose?

Better yet, avoid the school of hard knocks and give God a chance right now to bless you and take you on the right path to happiness. Without further ado, let the pursuit of real happiness begin!

2 – The Words of the Preacher

What is it worth to be able to read and learn from the compilations and experiences of the wisest and richest person who ever lived? What is it worth to be Solomon's disciple? Featured herein are:

1. The words of the wisest man who ever lived.
2. The words of the richest man who ever lived.
3. The words of the most powerful king in his days.
4. The words of the penitential sermon from the royal preacher.
5. The words of truth.

Ecclesiastes 1:1 The words of the Preacher, the son of David, king in Jerusalem.

Happiness is framed by the word of God. It begins with the word and it ends with the word in *Ecclesiastes 12*. There is no happiness outside of the word of God. Jesus Christ was the living Word; we now have the written Word.

Who is this person who calls himself a Preacher and makes the outrages claim of "vanity of vanities?" What is his résumé? Does he measure up to Socrates, Plato, or Aristotle?

He is the son of David and a king in Jerusalem. This Preacher is none other than King Solomon, who succeeded his father, King David, according to the account in *1Kings 1* and *1Kings 2*.

We have with us the words of the wisest man who ever lived. Solomon received a special gift of wisdom from God. *1Kings 3:12 Behold, I have done according to thy words: lo, I have given thee a wise and an understanding heart; so that there was none like thee before thee, neither after thee shall any arise like unto thee.* Read *1Kings 3:5-28, 1Kings 4:29-33, 1Kings 10:1-10.* Solomon immediately put the wisdom to work when he famously judged between two harlots who fought over a baby, according to *1Kings 3:16-28.*

We have with us the words of the richest man who ever lived. While there is no argument concerning Solomon's wisdom, people debate his wealth by comparing it with the wealth of the richest person in the world today. People like to calculate the value of Solomon's gold stockpile. A preacher once said Solomon's wealth makes the richest man in the world today look like he is on welfare. While Solomon's net worth is always up for debate, one thing we can hang our hat on is what God said of him.

Concerning Solomon's wealth, *2Chronicles 1:11 And God said to Solomon, Because this was in thine heart, and thou hast not asked riches, wealth, or honour, nor the life of thine enemies, neither yet hast asked long life; but hast asked wisdom and knowledge for thyself, that thou mayest judge my people, over whom I have made thee king: (12) Wisdom and knowledge is granted unto thee; and I will give thee riches, and wealth, and honour, such as none of the kings have had that have been before thee, neither shall there any after thee have the like.* Read *1Kings 4:20-28, 1Kings 9, 1Kings 10, 2Chronicles 9:27.*

One aspect that is overlooked is the purpose for Solomon's wisdom and wealth. God bestowed on him an extraordinary unique advantage and opportunity to study and experiment with life so that he could write it in the book of Ecclesiastes for the benefit of all. It is important that Solomon remains the wisest and richest man who ever lived so that no one can dispute his credibility. God will personally see to it that the records are not broken.

Ecclesiastes 1:12 I the Preacher was king over Israel in Jerusalem.

We have with us the words of the most powerful king in his day. Solomon was a powerful king over a vast domain, according to *1Kings 4:21, 24*. Israel was the world's superpower and the prestigious center of learning. Solomon received gifts and tributes from other kings. Essentially, he was a king of kings. Read *1Kings 9:11, 14-15, 1Kings 10:10-11, 14-15, 22-25*. Not surprisingly, there was no issue with peace in his kingdom. *1Kings 5:3 Thou knowest how that David my father could not build an house unto the name of the LORD his God for the wars which were about him on every side, until the LORD put them under the soles of his feet. (4) But now the LORD my God hath given me rest on every side, so that there is neither adversary nor evil occurrent.*

We also have with us the words of the penitential sermon from the royal Preacher, to which we ought to give heed, considering how God blessed him. It is interesting that Solomon not only never mentioned himself by name, he also declared that he *"was"* (past tense) the king over Israel, even though he never resigned or lost his kingship. He reigned in Jerusalem until the day he died, according to *1Kings 11:41, "And the rest of the acts of Solomon, and all that he did, and his wisdom, are they not written in the book of the acts of Solomon? (42) And the time that Solomon reigned in Jerusalem over all Israel was forty years. (43) And Solomon slept with his fathers, and was buried in the city of David his father: and Rehoboam his son reigned in his stead."* We also know that despite Solomon's sin, God did not remove the kingdom from him. *1Kings 11:34 Howbeit I will not take the whole kingdom out of his hand: but I will make him prince all the days of his life for David my servant's sake, whom I chose, because he kept my commandments and my statutes: (35) But I will take the kingdom out of his son's hand, and will give it unto thee, even ten tribes.*

It could be that Solomon wrote the book of Ecclesiastes to be published and read after his death. The name Solomon means peace. Perhaps the reason Solomon concealed his name was because of his apostasy (*1Kings 11:1-13*), in that by departing from God, he lost his peace. He might have privately resigned as king and took on the role of a preacher, as someone who had been brought to repentance and resolved to teach others God's way like his father David in *Psalms 51:13, "Then will I teach transgressors thy ways; and sinners shall be converted unto thee."* Indeed, the hope of every preacher is that his sermons will outlive him and have an eternal impact.

Finally, we have with us the words of truth that can make us wise and live a happy life. *Ecclesiastes 12:10 The preacher sought to find out acceptable words: and that which was written was upright, even words of truth.* Nobles and aristocrats from all over the world went to Jerusalem to hear Solomon's wisdom. *1Kings 4:34 And there came of all people to hear the wisdom of Solomon, from all kings of the earth, which had heard of his wisdom. 1Kings 10:24 And all the earth sought to Solomon, to hear his wisdom, which God had put in his heart.* If we lived in Solomon's time, how likely is it that we would be invited to his palace to hear his wisdom? What would be our chances of getting a copy of his writings?

There is no doubt Solomon was wiser, richer, more powerful, and more experienced than Socrates, Plato, and Aristotle. More importantly, Solomon had wisdom that God put in his heart, according to *1Kings 10:24*. This means we have access to the mind of God and the learned lessons and instructions from Solomon.

Solomon is a type of Christ in several ways:

Solomon	Jesus Christ
Preacher	*Matthew 4:17 From that time Jesus began to <u>preach</u>, and to say, Repent: for the kingdom of heaven is at hand.*
Son of David	*Matthew 9:27 And when Jesus departed thence, two blind men followed him, crying, and saying, Thou <u>Son of David</u>, have mercy on us.*
Peace	*Isaiah 9:6 For unto us a child is born, unto us a son is given: and the government shall be upon his shoulder: and his name shall be called Wonderful, Counsellor, The mighty God, The everlasting Father, The <u>Prince of Peace</u>.*
King of the Jews	*Matthew 2:1 Now when Jesus was born in Bethlehem of Judaea in the days of Herod the king, behold, there came wise men from the east to Jerusalem, (2) Saying, Where is he that is born <u>King of the Jews</u>? for we have seen his star in the east, and are come to worship him.*
King of a vast domain	*Isaiah 9:7 Of the increase of his government and peace <u>there shall be no end</u>, upon the throne of David, and upon his kingdom, to order it, and to establish it with judgment and with justice from henceforth even for ever. The zeal of the LORD of hosts will perform this.*
King of kings	*Revelation 19:16 And he hath on his vesture and on his thigh a name written, <u>KING OF KINGS</u>, AND LORD OF LORDS.*
King who received gifts and tributes from other kings	*Zechariah 14:16 And it shall come to pass, that every one that is left of <u>all the nations</u> which came against Jerusalem shall even go up from year to year <u>to worship the King</u>, the LORD of hosts, and to keep the feast of tabernacles.*
	Revelation 21:24 And the nations of them which

> *are saved shall walk in the light of it: and the* <u>*kings of the earth do bring their glory and honour into it*</u>*.*

The wisest man

> *Ro 11:33 O the depth of the riches both of the wisdom and knowledge of God! how unsearchable are his judgments, and his ways past finding out!*

> *1Corinthians 1:24 But unto them which are called, both Jews and Greeks, Christ the power of God, and the wisdom of God.*

> *Colossians 2:3 In whom are hid all the treasures of wisdom and knowledge.*

The richest man

> *Ephesians 3:8 Unto me, who am less than the least of all saints, is this grace given, that I should preach among the Gentiles the unsearchable riches of Christ.*

Historically, the *"Preacher"* in verses 1 and 12 was Solomon, a king who turned preacher. What caused the wisest, richest, and most powerful king to despair of the world and declare himself a preacher when others go the opposite direction and strive to own the world to become a king in their domain?

Doctrinally, the *"Preacher"* points to the Master, Rabbi, who is the Lord Jesus Christ. Read *Matthew 8:19*.

Spiritually, the *"Preacher"* is every born-again believer, according to *2Timothy 4:1-2.* Every Christian should *"preach the word; be instant in season, out of season; reprove, rebuke, exhort with all longsuffering and doctrine."* Wise children of God despair of the world and give themselves to spiritual work.

3 – Vanity of Human Courses Under the Sun

I f I were a rich man, I would buy you a ticket on the SpaceX Dragon spaceship and transport you to live on a beautiful blue planet. I should give you some information before you go.

You will be transformed in many ways once you enter the planet's atmosphere. Most importantly, you will not come out alive. Life is hard, and you will labor tirelessly for meaningless things. Life is also short, uncertain, and empty; and the emptiness is so painful that you may consider suicide. You will search for happiness in the wrong things, and all your efforts will be in vain. Forget happiness. Your best advantage in life is found in eating, drinking, and making merry, and you will gain nothing from a lifetime of labor.

No worries, I am not a rich man, so I will not be buying you the ticket. But oh wait, how did you get here already? Well then, welcome to beautiful planet Earth. Your welcome packet is filled with wonderful things to get you started and help you navigate life in this world. It also includes a bowl of cherries and a photo book to capture the sweet memories of your sojourn. Two full-time butlers (parents) are assigned to you for the first 18 years of your life. Enjoy life immediately and make a difference!

Okay, that is a stretch. You already realize that life isn't rainbows and butterflies, and you may still be working on catching the ever elusive happiness. You may be seeking relief in the fleeting quick fixes of the world. If so, no wonder you are unhappy. Anyone who seeks fulfillment from the world is guaranteed disappointment.

Featured herein are the opening paragraphs of the book of Ecclesiastes comprising of a proclamation, a question, and philosophical proofs to show the vanity of human courses under the sun.

Ecclesiastes 1:2 Vanity of vanities, saith the Preacher, vanity of vanities; all is vanity.

Now that you have landed on planet Earth, the first thing you'll need to know is that this world is the *"vanity of vanities."* Not just vanity, but vanity of the worst kind. In case it is unclear, *"vanity of vanities"* is repeated in the same short verse for confirmation, intensity, and attention. The sentiment of this verse is ominous, and it means this world is void of happiness. It is vanity in totality—*"all is vanity."*

If you ever wonder why life can be so empty and meaningless, it is because you are in the "vanity of vanities!" Searching for happiness in this world is as silly as trying to find a warm spot in a freezer running at full blast.

There is nothing a self-serving person (Christian or otherwise) can do to be happy in this world. All the individual's pursuits of happiness are vain. Self-serving people don't have to believe it, but they will certainly feel the pain of emptiness.

Welcome to the "vanity of vanities!"

Billions of people are barking up the wrong tree (the world) hoping for happiness that doesn't exist. Sadly, they reject the one tree that produces the fruit of true happiness—the tree of life (Jesus Christ). The formula is simple: Hope – Reality = Frustration.

There is a huge disparity between God's view and man's view of this world. We see it as a place to enjoy, invest our lives, and build our dreams. God sees it as the vanity of vanities—an utterly worthless place. Until we see this world as God sees it, we will be captivated by it and will set our affections on things that lead to emptiness and unhappiness. God's counsel in *Colossians 3:1* says, *"If ye then be risen with Christ, seek those things which are above, where Christ sitteth on the right hand of God. (2) Set your affection on things above, not on things on the earth."* We are to have a single affection—an overriding affection of all affections—for the celestial things above, valuing them more than the treasures of the world. But many of us reject this counsel and seek happiness from the world instead.

God and the devil not only battle for the souls of people, they also battle for their affections. It is not surprising for people who are without Christ to live for self and seek happiness from the world, because they have no hope beyond this life. But it is unacceptable for believers in Jesus Christ to not serve Him and to set their affections on terrestrial things. *Psalms 73:3 For I was envious at the foolish, when I saw the prosperity of the wicked.* Read *Psalms 73.*

It is important to note that God did not intend for the earth to be a place of futility, emptiness, and hopelessness. It became this way through sin, beginning with Lucifer's rebellion. *Jeremiah 4:23 I beheld the earth, and, lo, it was without form, and void; and the heavens, and they had no light.* The phrase *"without form"* is also translated as *"vanity."* The word *"void"* is also translated as *"emptiness."*

Does it take a genius to sense the emptiness in this world? Anyone who seeks happiness from this world realizes that this world is jacked up and that its ability to yield happiness is slim to none, and slim has left the room.

Hello happiness seekers, meet emptiness.

Worldly satisfaction and happiness are emptiness in disguise that will hurt you. They are like cotton candy, which looks colorful and tasty at first, but is reduced to nothing in a moment and leaves a sticky mess.

Imagine a beautifully decorated cookie tin on top of a high cabinet with the slogan, "Happiness is a warm cookie." The cookies pictured on the tin look so delicious. Your brain says, "Give me the whole tin!" But you hear, "Psst, it's an empty tin," from a Bible on the counter. You refuse to believe. You get a step ladder and go for the cookies, only to find an empty tin. How disappointing! Such is the experience of everyone who refuses to heed the Bible and falls for the world's deception.

The world wraps itself with lies that are so tempting. Only the word of God can expose the world for what it really is—vanity of vanities.

The emptiness is so depressively painful that some people practice self-mutilation by cutting, because it is less painful. The pain of emptiness is permanently carved into their skin. A young man from my church who cut himself before knowing Jesus Christ said, "My therapist pointed me to a psychiatrist, and the psychiatrist pointed me to drugs. And when drugs pointed to nothing, I gave up on hope." His was diagnosed and treated as if he was a bag of chemicals and not a human with a soul and a spirit. Thank God, someone pointed him to Jesus Christ, and he is healed.

"Over the past two decades, the use of antidepressants has skyrocketed. One in 10 Americans now takes an antidepressant medication; among women in their 40s and 50s, the figure is one in four," according to an article in "The New York Times."

Many famous superstars and successful people commit suicide because after working so hard for years to reach the top, they discover exactly what the Bible says, *"Vanity of vanities."* They find success does not translate to happiness, and they remain empty, hopeless, and unfulfilled. Depression sets in, and many turn to alcohol and cannabis and opioid products to numb and kill the pain. (How can success be so painful? What happened to sweet success?) When drugs and alcohol deliver addiction instead of a real fix, the users despair and give up on life. A bumper sticker says, "Life sucks, then you die." According to "USA Today", as many as 40,000 people commit suicide annually in the U.S. The suicide rate is also increasing across all age and gender groups, according to a report by the National Center for Health Statistics, while behavioral scientists debate whether this is a mental or a public health problem.

Ecclesiastes 1:3 What profit hath a man of all his labour which he taketh under the sun?

Following the shocking proclamation in verse 2, this verse questions and challenges the capacity of human labor in securing happiness in this world under the sun. It is human nature to rely on self to secure happiness through one's ingenuity, ability, effort, and cunningness. God challenges people to show one thing that they can do to be truly happy without accepting His Son Jesus Christ as Lord and Savior and serving Him. Go ahead, have it your way, take your best shot at being happy on your own and see how life will work out for you.

Consider *Isaiah 50:10, "Who is among you that feareth the LORD, that obeyeth the voice of his servant, that walketh in darkness, and hath no light? let him trust in the name of the LORD, and stay upon his God. (11) Behold, all ye that kindle a fire, that compass yourselves about with sparks: walk in the light of your fire, and in the sparks that ye have kindled. This shall ye have of mine hand; ye shall lie down in sorrow."* To those who fear God and obey the words of His Servant (Jesus Christ), but are presently in darkness (state of unhappiness), let them hope in the trustworthy name of Jehovah and lean on Him, for He will turn their mourning into dancing. But those who choose to manufacture happiness their way and rejoice in the sparks of their self effort will remain in sorrow. Man's way leads to a hopeless end, but God's way leads to an endless hope.

If you ever wonder why you remain empty and can't seem to find happiness no matter what you do, that's by design. But if you believe there is a God and a hereafter, what are you doing living for self and chasing after worldly happiness, which is an oxymoron?

What are you laboring toward in hope of happiness? What things from the menu below do you hope will make you happy?

Double Happiness Menu

Riches & Possessions
Knowledge
Sensual Pleasures
Worldly Success
Power
Combo – Bucks, Babes, Big toys

When you get the things you want, do they bring real and lasting happiness or are you still unsatisfied? The subsequent chapters in this book will debunk the idea of worldly things offering lasting happiness. So, what profit is there in laboring for things that do not satisfy and that you can't take with you in the afterlife?

God just exploded two bombshells before you: 1) You are in the vanity of vanities; 2) There is nothing you can do to be happy on your own.

As an adult who has been educated by the world and relied on self and worldly methods for happiness, it is hard to fathom this world that you affectionately call home all of a sudden is the vanity of vanities. You probably disagree with the word of God and still think that there are multiple ways to happiness. Your affections remain on the things of the world, and you enjoy living for self. If so, you are about to see your deal under the sun.

The next four verses enlist the testimonies of four witnesses. They are not humans, but are natural phenomena of God's creation. They are mortality, sun, wind, and rivers. As in the game of charades, they will act out the words "brevity," "restless," "uncertain," and "unfulfilling," respectively. Furthermore, each natural phenomenon illustrates the vanity of human courses under the sun with three attributes: a fixed circuit, a transitory nature, and never-ending labor.

Ecclesiastes 1:4 One generation passeth away, and another generation cometh: but the earth abideth for ever.

Whenever I am at a graveyard, I like to survey the age of the deceased by the years inscribed on their tombstones—the year they were born and the year they died, separated by a little dash. I conclude that life is nothing more than a short dash that encapsulates a lifetime of labor. It doesn't matter who the person is. The lifetime and achievements of the greatest dad, the most wonderful mom, the richest person, and the poorest peasant is represented by a short dash when it is all said and done. The wise and the fool are no different. What a vanity! *Psalms 144:4 Man is like to vanity: his days are as a shadow that passeth away.* Read *Job 14:1-2, Psalms 39:5, Psalms 62:9, Psalms 103:15-16, Isaiah 40:17.*

The subject of death is taboo in my Asian culture, especially in my parents' generation. In many parts of Asia, people still make a spitting sound or say something similar to "be it far from me" when they see a hearse, a coffin, or a dead person. A life insurance sales person would never say, "What happens if you die today?" He would get kicked out. In this superstitious culture, it is not acceptable to mention death or make any reference to it on such auspicious occasions as Chinese New Year, weddings, and birthdays. White and black colors are also forbidden at such occasions, as they represent death and sorrow. Red, green, yellow, and blue are acceptable colors representing blood, life, prosperity, and heaven. Clueless Western tourists who purchase white lanterns for decoration, not knowing that they are used in funerals, always make me chuckle.

Ancient Egyptian pharaohs and Chinese emperors went to great lengths to secure their afterlife. They were buried with treasures and things they thought were needed for the afterlife. What happened to those things? Some treasures were stolen by grave robbers. Some were uncovered by archeologists and are displayed in museums. The rest remains to be discovered. The largest pottery figurine group ever found in China is the Terracotta Army consisting of over 8,000 warriors, 130 chariots, and 670 horses. One thing is for sure—none were able to take anything with them. What a bummer! *Ecclesiastes 5:15 As he came forth of his mother's womb, naked shall he return to go as he came, and shall take nothing of his labour, which he may carry away in his hand.* (There is a way to convert earthly treasures into heavenly treasures. This is covered in the Vanity of Wealth chapter.)

My perspective on death has changed since I became a Christian. Death is no longer a taboo subject, but is a finish line because I have hope beyond this life. *2Corinthians 4:18 While we look not at the things which are seen, but at the things which are not seen: for the things which are seen are temporal; but the things which are not seen are eternal.* My focus and affections are on things above the sun. There are at least four things that are worthy of my affections and investment:

1. The person of God
2. The Word of God
3. The kingdom of God
4. The people of God

These will endure for eternity, and my investment in them will pay dividends in the afterlife. *Matthew 6:19 Lay not up for yourselves treasures upon earth, where moth and rust doth corrupt, and where thieves break through and steal: (20) But lay up for yourselves treasures in heaven, where neither moth nor rust doth corrupt, and where thieves do not break through nor steal: (21) For where your treasure is, there will your heart be also.*

In *Ecclesiastes 1:4,* mortality acts out its charade word, **"brevity,"** to show the vanity of life on earth.

- Observe the fixed circuit of life.
  All life on earth runs on a one-way circuit between two nodes originating with birth and terminating with death, and no one can alter the course. Humans are on a fixed collision course with death the moment they are born, and no one will come out alive. *Ecclesiastes 8:8a There is no man that hath power over the spirit to retain the spirit; neither hath he power in the day of death: and there is no discharge in that war.* Death is a stinky deal.

- Observe the transitory nature of life on earth.
  It is a short circuit. New births usher in a new generation that replaces the outgoing because of mortality. No amount of physical exercise, healthy eating, anti-aging foods, supplemental vitamins, stem cell transplants, or geographic relocation can deliver a person from death. The short tenure of life in each generation limits enjoyment. Humans are inferior to the dirt (earth) that they trample under their feet. *"The earth abideth for ever,"* but humans are visitors. The dirt has seen

generations of human visitors come and go, never to return.

- Observe the restless labor that does not benefit the worker in the end.
  It is a laborious circuit. Life is laborious with no end to human labor, yet no one can take anything away. The fruit of the labor can only be enjoyed while the person is alive and healthy.

Given the above, anyone who labors for self in the vanity of vanities is subject to the following labor conditions:

1. You will soon be removed and replaced.
2. You can take nothing with you when you are replaced.

How are these labor conditions good for anyone? Would you be excited if you got this job offer: "Congratulations, you are hired. You should know that the company loves a hard-working employee. You are welcome to enjoy whatever your salary affords. But you should also know that the company can terminate your employment at any time, and when it happens, all your savings and everything you own returns to the company."?

Would you set your affections on this company? Of course not. You would say, "I am out of here!"

The antidote for the brevity of life in this world is to accept the gift of God, which is eternal life. *Romans 6:23 For the wages of sin is death; but the gift of God is eternal life through Jesus Christ our Lord.* This means by faith accept Jesus Christ as Lord and Savior for the pardoning of your sins. Happy is the person whose sins are forgiven and has obtained eternal life. *Psalms 32:1 Blessed is he whose transgression is forgiven, whose sin is covered.*

Your salvation is the beginning of happiness and a new life in Christ. The chain of sin is broken, and you no longer have to serve sin. Read *Romans 6*. Your next steps are to learn the Bible, be discipled, and serve the Lord. The only way you can keep the fruits of your labor is to serve Him. You will have an account with God in heaven and will be able to access it when you get there.

Ecclesiastes 1:5 The sun also ariseth, and the sun goeth down, and hasteth to his place where he arose.

The spectacular sunrise atop the Haleakala volcano in Maui is an unforgettable enchanting experience that should be on everyone's "1,000 places to see before you die" list. Be prepared however to rise at 3 a.m. or earlier, drive two hours up a curvy mountain road in a convoy of slow cars in darkness and brave the cold and windy conditions at the summit, which is over 10,000 feet above sea level. The anticipation of seeing the first sign of the sun generates much thrill and excitement. The exuberant energy can be felt in the air. As soon as the tip of the sun breaks the horizon, the crowd cheers and claps. Some kiss, propose, or praise God for the new day. The colors of the sky are amazing as the dark gray, blue, and magenta colors make room for orange. Within minutes, the sun is fully risen. E ala e! (Hawaiian for Awaken!) Moments later, the sun is too bright for the naked eye.

New life on earth is much like the rising sun. It is full of anticipation and labor, yet is beautiful. The baby will soon be a toddler, then walking and running in the blink of an eye. And just as if it was yesterday, the child will rise to the most prominent and glorious position in life as the brightest noon sun—full of strength and beauty. The "Sunrise, Sunset" song from the Broadway Musical "Fiddler on the roof" says it well.

Is this the little girl I carried?
Is this the little boy at play?
I don't remember growing older
When did they?

When did she get to be a beauty?
When did he grow to be so tall?
Wasn't it yesterday
When they were small?

Sunrise, sunset (2X)
Swiftly flow the days.
Seedlings turn overnight to sunflowers,
Blossoming even as we gaze.

Sunrise, sunset (2X)
Swiftly fly the years.
One season following another,
Laden with happiness and tears.

In *Ecclesiastes 1:5*, the sun acts out its charade word
"**restless**," to show the vanity of life on earth. The rising and setting
of the sun represents a person's lifecycle.

- Observe the fixed circuit.
  The sun is locked in a fixed circuit. It rises from the east
  and goes down to the west. This parallels the one-way
  circuit of human life that starts with birth and ends with
  death.

- Observe the transitory nature.
  There are only a few hours of daylight each day. How
  quickly the sun sets after it rises. This parallels the short
  human lifespan.

  It also shows that no one can remain in life's prominent
  position. We will all soon find ourselves setting like the
  sun, and death will come to rush us along. The season of
  glory days is so short that it is omitted from the verse—
  "*The sun also ariseth, and the sun goeth down.*" There is
  no mention of the mid-day glory of the sun. Notice the

comma after the word "ariseth." This means after a short pause or season in the limelight, life begins to go downhill like a setting sun. Read *Jeremiah 9:23-24, 1Peter 1:24-25*. It takes so much time to ramp up and be successful in life, and once we get there, not only does it not satisfy, it soon is time to wrap up life. A message on a 40th birthday card says, "Congratulations, you have the best surround view" with a stick figure person standing on the pinnacle of a hill. We all know that surround view will soon turn into a scary down slope.

Time flies so fast, it scares me. I find myself saying "Can you believe this is already...?" Months disappear just like that. Indeed, one season follows another, and how swiftly fly the years!

- Observe the restless labor that does not benefit the worker in the end.
Like humans, the sun also has a laborious circuit. The sun labors everyday to produce brilliant light and heat, yet it gets absolutely no profit from past productions. The next day is the next incarnation, and the sun has no choice but to repeat the same laborious cycle every day. As the saying goes, "Same stuff, different day". The cycle is unstoppable, and there is no rest for the weary sun as the word *"hasteth"* in verse 5 suggests. After setting, the sun rushes to rise again, but only to find itself in the same place it started yesterday—back to square one and no closer to happiness. This parallels human lives on earth. Life exists briefly in a circuit that is full of labor. Every person in every generation is subject to the same vanity. Everyone must labor, but gains nothing in the end. Once our sun sets, it is game over. We die and become worm chow. Unlike the sun, we will not rise again. We are done. We leave everything behind, and

our souls face judgment. We get one pass with no second chance or reincarnation. Our best case is to go out at a ripe old age, but there is no guarantee whatsoever that we will.

Life in the vanity of vanities has to be depressing for people whose affections are on the things of this world. This applies to non-Christians and Christians who do not serve God. The more they have of the world, the more they have to manage and the more restless and depressed they will be, especially in their twilight years.

Tired of a restless life? The antidote is to rest in Jesus Christ. *Matthew 11:28 Come unto me, all ye that labour and are heavy laden, and I will give you rest. (29) Take my yoke upon you, and learn of me; for I am meek and lowly in heart: and ye shall find rest unto your souls.* Verse 28 says, *"Come unto me..."* This means accepting Jesus Christ as Lord and Savior. Verse 29 says, *"Take my yoke upon you..."* This is serving the Lord. Outside of this, there is no rest. The first mention of the word "rest" in the Bible is in *Genesis 8:9, "But the dove found no rest for the sole of her foot, and she returned unto him into the ark, for the waters were on the face of the whole earth: then he put forth his hand, and took her, and pulled her in unto him into the ark."* Notice there is no rest in this world.

Ecclesiastes 1:6 The wind goeth toward the south, and turneth about unto the north; it whirleth about continually, and the wind returneth again according to his circuits.

Not to be outdone by the sun, the wind also acts out its charade word, "**uncertain**," to substantiate the vanity of life on earth.

- Observe the fixed circuit.
  The wind is locked in a fixed circuit that goes from north to south. The American English slang "go south" is not a

good thing. It means to decline or fall in value. This parallels the one-way circuit of human life going from birth to death.

- Observe the transitory nature.
  The wind whirls about perpetually and does not remain in one place for too long. This parallels the brevity of human life on earth.

- Observe the restless labor that does not benefit the worker in the end.
  Like humans, the wind also has a laborious circuit. Much energy is spent on blowing and whirling in every season, yet the wind gets no benefits from its labor from the previous season. The cycle is unstoppable, and the entire course is repeated in the next season. This parallels the vanity of human labor on earth. Every generation begins the same, toils through a lifetime of labor, ends the same, and is no closer to happiness.

Life on earth is not as easy as the gentle breeze of the old Irish blessing—"May the wind always be at your back." It can be twisty and violent as a whirlwind that destroys, limits enjoyment, and increases vanity and misery. There is no guarantee we can amass the nest eggs that will see us through the golden years. Bad things such as accidents, sickness, theft, war, acts of government, acts of God, etc., could wipe out everything we work so hard to own and enjoy. And we have to start over. *Job 14:1 Man that is born of a woman is of few days, and full of trouble.*

Life happens so fast and sometimes violently, and keeps us constantly spinning in different directions emotionally, mentally, spiritually, and physically. We may find ourselves in a whirlwind after receiving a phone call about a loved one suddenly taken to the hospital emergency room. The whirlwind grows larger and stronger and feels like an F5 tornado with each subsequent phone call of bad news. Or the whirlwind may begin at the workplace with news of a layoff. There is no peace in this world, and life is full of adversities. Real peace is in Jesus Christ. Read *John 14:27*. Would you face your whirlwinds alone without help from Christ? *Isaiah 40:31 But they that wait upon the LORD shall renew their strength; they shall mount up with wings as eagles; they shall run, and not be weary; and they shall walk, and not faint.*

Life is uncertain, but the word of God is sure. We can take it to the bank. *Proverbs 22:21 That I might make thee know the certainty of the words of truth; that thou mightest answer the words of truth to them that send unto thee? 2Peter 1:19 We have also a more sure word of prophecy; whereunto ye do well that ye take heed, as unto a light that shineth in a dark place, until the day dawn, and the day star arise in your hearts.* We combat uncertainty by living His certain word. It boils down to trust and obey. *Matthew 4:4 But he answered and said, It is written, Man shall not live by bread alone, but by every word that proceedeth out of the mouth of God.*

The wind has a north-south circuit, while the sun takes the east-west course. Together, they form the Calvary cross, cover the four corners of the earth, and blanket the world with the message of vanity. We cannot plead ignorance. God, through the elements of His creation, daily reminds us of the vanity under the sun and the answer in Jesus Christ. "At the cross, at the cross where I first saw the light, And the burden of my heart rolled away, It was there by faith I received my sight, And now I am happy all the day"—Lyrics from the hymn "At the Cross" by Isaac Watts.

Ecclesiastes 1:7 All the rivers run into the sea; yet the sea is not full; unto the place from whence the rivers come, thither they return again.

My personal favorite is the illustration of rivers that have tried in vain to fill the ocean since the day they were created.

The rivers represent such never-ending worldly feeds of satisfaction and happiness as rivers of delight, pleasure, prosperity, longevity, serenity, supremacy, splendor, opulence, and so on. The phrase *"all the rivers"* means everything is covered—every possible thing humans can discover, develop, make, invent, improve, advance, move, or replace to make them happy. All worldly employments and pleasures will never yield happiness and fulfillment, because they simply do not have it in them. You can't squeeze blood out of a turnip.

The sea represents the human body, which can never be full or satisfied by the things of the world. It will always be troubled and restless.

You can own multiple multi-million dollar mansions and still not be satisfied. You can have the biggest and baddest toys in the world and still not be satisfied. When was the last time a worldly thing brought you lasting happiness? You get nothing by placing your hope in and pursuing after things that do not satisfy. This world is like a giant hamster wheel for people who chase after worldly satisfaction and happiness.

Happiness sought through drugs evaporates when the effects wear off. The highs are intense, but the lows and withdrawals are unbearable. The first high is euphoric, but subsequent highs are not as satisfying. Happiness is still as far away as ever. As rivers erode their banks, drug abusers' lives also erode as they continue down the destructive psychedelic path. The same goes for abuse of alcohol, sex, food, money, etc.

The rivers and sea jointly act out the charade word, **"unfulfilling,"** to illustrate the vanity of life on earth.

- Observe the fixed circuit.

The rivers are locked in a fixed circuit that goes from the high-elevation headwaters to the sea. This one-way flow parallels the downhill flow of human life from birth to death.

- Observe the transitory nature.
  The water flows nonstop from the headwaters to the sea. The journey is quick. This parallels the brevity of human life on earth.

- Observe the restless labor that does not benefit the worker in the end.
  The rivers have labored restlessly to fill the oceans for thousands of years, yet the oceans are never full. The discharge rate from the Amazon River alone is over 7 million cubic feet per second. The liquid from the headwaters belongs to the perpetual hydrological cycle. It quickly evaporates from the sea, condenses to form precipitation in the atmosphere, falls on the earth, and runs back to the sea. Read *Psalms 135:7*. All the labor of filling the sea is for nothing. It is like pouring water into a bottomless glass. This parallels the vanity of human labor on earth. No amount of worldly feeds can satisfy the body, and we are no closer to happiness.

Tired of an unfulfilled life? Stop quenching your thirsty soul with the world's water and switch to Jesus' water. Jesus instructed the Samaritan woman as such: *John 4:13 Jesus answered and said unto her, Whosoever drinketh of this water shall thirst again: (14) But whosoever drinketh of the water that I shall give him shall never thirst; but the water that I shall give him shall be in him a well of water springing up into everlasting life.* As water is a type of the word of God, according to *Ephesians 5:25-26*, this means we should live by God's words in order to be satisfied and happy. *Isaiah 55:1 Ho, every one that thirsteth, come ye to the waters, and he that hath no money; come ye, buy, and eat; yea, come, buy wine and milk without money and without price. (2) Wherefore do ye spend money for that which is not bread? and your labour for that which satisfieth not? hearken diligently unto me, and eat ye that which is good, and let your soul delight itself in fatness. (3) Incline your ear, and come unto me: hear, and your soul shall live; and I will make an everlasting covenant with you, even the sure mercies of David.*

Go online and listen to the hymn "Fill my cup, Lord" by Richard Blanchard.

Like the woman at the well, I was seeking
For things that could not satisfy.
And then I heard my Savior speaking:
"Draw from My well that never shall run dry."

Chorus:
Fill my cup, Lord;
I lift it up Lord;
Come and quench this thirsting of my soul.
Bread of Heaven, feed me till I want no more.
Fill my cup, fill it up and make me whole.

There are millions in this world who are seeking
For pleasures earthly goods afford.
But none can match the wondrous treasure
That I find in Jesus Christ my Lord.

So my brother if the things that this world gives you
Leave hungers that won't pass away,
My blessed Lord will come and save you
If you kneel to Him and humbly pray.

Note:

Bible students would appreciate that the sun is a type of the Lord Jesus Christ. Notice the sun has the *"he"* pronoun in verse 5. Also notice the phrase *"to his place where he arose,"* which points to the *"tabernacle for the sun"* in *Psalms 19*. Read *Psalms 19:1-6*. The wind is a type of the Holy Ghost. Notice the *"his"* pronoun in verse 6. Read *John 3:5-8*. The water is a type of the Word, who is God, according to *John 1:1*. Read *Ephesians 5:25-26.* Collectively, they represent the Holy Trinity.

The chart below summarizes the lessons from the four witnesses:

Witness	Fixed Circuit	Short Circuit	Zero-gain Laborious Circuit	Message
Mortality	Birth . . . Death	"One generation passeth away, and another generation cometh: but the earth abideth for ever." • A lifespan is so short. The dirt we trample under our feet will outlast us.	Life is laborious, yet can take nothing away.	Life is short.
Sun	East . . . West	"The sun also ariseth, and the sun goeth down..." • Only a few hours of daylight.	"...and hasteth to his place where he arose" – laborious. • Back to square one – no closer to happiness.	Life is restless.
Wind	North . . . South	"The wind goeth toward the south, and turneth about unto the north..." • A short trip from north to south.	"...it whirleth about continually, and the wind returneth again according to his circuits" – laborious. • Back to square one – no closer to happiness.	Life is uncertain.
River	Headwater. .Sea	"All the rivers run into the sea; yet the sea is not full..." • A short trip from the headwater to the river delta and sea.	"...unto the place from whence the rivers come, thither they return again" – laborious. • Back to square one – no closer to happiness.	Life is unfulfilling.

The wisest man has proclaimed. God's witnesses have spoken, yet some are still not convinced that this world is the vanity of vanities and happiness is in Jesus Christ only. They want to live for self and trust in human power to bring about happiness.

The next four verses explain why it is impossible for us to be content and happy on our own. There are three monsters, courtesy of God, that drive us absolutely restless and unhappy.

Ecclesiastes 1:8 All things are full of labour; man cannot utter it: the eye is not satisfied with seeing, nor the ear filled with hearing.

Where do we even begin to describe how laborious life is! There is so much to do and so little time to enjoy. We have to work for everything, yet we are not satisfied with the things we gain from our labor. Many things end up in garage sales.

Adam was sent to hard labor when he was kicked out of Eden. *Genesis 3:17 And unto Adam he said, Because thou hast hearkened unto the voice of thy wife, and hast eaten of the tree, of which I commanded thee, saying, Thou shalt not eat of it: cursed is the ground for thy sake; in sorrow shalt thou eat of it all the days of thy life; (18) Thorns also and thistles shall it bring forth to thee; and thou shalt eat the herb of the field; (19) In the sweat of thy face shalt thou eat bread, till thou return unto the ground; for out of it wast thou taken: for dust thou art, and unto dust shalt thou return.*

Subsequently, all Adam's descendants who inherit his sin nature are also subject to the same punishment. Hence Solomon's question is, *"What profit hath a man of all his labour...,"* instead of "What profit hath a man of all his enjoyment...?" All who come into this world must serve the sentence of their sin. Life is so laborious that any enjoyment it brings is so disproportionate to the amount of labor required to obtain it. It's like a pound of labor for an ounce of pleasure. Working all year for a week-long fun vacation is not a good deal, is it? Are you checking and responding to work emails while on vacation?

The eyes and ears are the insatiable monsters of our natural bodies that drive us to endless labor, magnifying our affliction. They are the taskmasters for which we toil. We have more things than ever, yet we rarely find time to enjoy them, because we are working on getting the next thing that promises to make us look more cool, hip, and sexy. Case in point, many of us wouldn't be caught dead driving a no-flash, out-of-style station wagon or a minivan, because we would look better in a trendy SUV.

"The eye is not satisfied with seeing"—how many times can we watch the same movie before our eyes become dissatisfied and demand to change the channel? How long can we play with the same toy, drive the same car, or live in the same house before our eyes catch something newer, shinier, faster, nicer, or more elegant, making us discontent with what we already have? And so we labor for the new thing. *Proverbs 27:20* says the eyes are like the consuming hell fire that cannot be satisfied.

"Nor the ear filled with hearing"—how many times can we listen to the same song, story, or news before our ears say, "Tell me something I don't already know"? Ever wonder why the music and movie industries are so successful?

Our eyes and ears cannot be satisfied as they drive us to toil for things that are inconsequential in the afterlife. As such, we are continually restless. Our dissatisfactions drive innovations, new industries, demands, and the global economy that powers the world. All the labor makes us very busy, tired, and miserable, and at the end of the day, still unsatisfied.

Ecclesiastes 1:9 The thing that hath been, it is that which shall be; and that which is done is that which shall be done: and there is no new thing under the sun. (10) Is there any thing whereof it may be said, See, this is new? it hath been already of old time, which was before us. (11) There is no remembrance of former things; neither shall there be any remembrance of things that are to come with those that shall come after.

Worse than insatiable desires driven by the eye and ear, our short and unreliable memory causes us to repeat the same foolish things in every generation. How easily and quickly we forget what we know.

Humans have labored for satisfaction and happiness under the sun since the day Adam was kicked out of Eden. No one has ever found solid and substantial happiness in living for self in this world. Yet every new generation thinks they are smarter and more advanced. In reality they repeat the same failed practices and work like a dog for temporal enjoyments and creature comforts.

Everything that we could possibly do for happiness in living for self has been tried by previous generations. And what we do for happiness today will be imitated by future generations who will think they discovered the holy grail of happiness. When people say, *"See, this is new,"* as in a new discovery or way of happiness, don't buy it. The thing has been chewed over before. It is a recycled failed practice. Don't be a sucker.

The reason failed practices of old can reappear as new is because our memory fails us—*"there is no remembrance of former things."* The reason failed practices will live on in future generations, as much as we try to warn them, is because of the same shortcoming of the creature—*"neither shall there be any remembrance of things that are to come with those that shall come after."* Hence the idiom, "What's old is new again...and again, and again."

The truth is, *"there is no new thing under the sun."* To hope for happiness in self-serving is to deny the obvious in the face of all evidence to the contrary. Let's say you trust in riches for happiness, and so you work for it. Along the way, you learn of millionaires who committed suicide because of depression. Yet somehow you think you are different, and you chalk their depression up to some sort of disease. Why bet on a hope that has proven to fail?

Go online and listen to the hymn "I've discovered the way of gladness" by Floyd W. Hawkins.

> Mankind is searching ev'ry day,
> In quest of something new;
> But I have found the "Living Way,"
> The path of pleasures true.
>
> Chorus
> I've discovered the way of gladness
> I've discovered the way of joy
> I've discovered relief from sadness
> 'Tis a happiness without alloy;
> I've discovered the fount of blessings,
> I've discovered the "Living Word"
> 'Twas the greatest of all discoveries,
> When I found Jesus my Lord.
>
> I've found the Pearl of greatest price,
> "Eternal life" so fair;
> 'Twas through the Savior's sacrifice,
> I found this jewel rare.

Final Thoughts

Mankind has a problem. We are in the vanity of vanities, a place void of happiness. The solution is to accept Jesus Christ as Lord and Savior, and serve Him.

The four natural phenomena reveal the vanity of human courses under the sun through their charades that encourage people to despair of worldly affections. Mortality says, "Life is too short to waste it on meaningless and inconsequential things." The sun says, "Life is restless." The wind says, "Life is uncertain." The river says, "Life is unfulfilling." Humans are inferior to nature in that we die, never to return again, but nature retraces its courses.

We also learn that our felicity rests not in the human creature, because it cannot be satisfied. To be happy on our own, we must be able to arrive at contentment, which is impossible without Christ. The eyes and ears cannot be satisfied and will drive us ever restlessly for inconsequential things. One can have the most of everything and still want more when the heart and mind are not set on Christ.

Hello self-serving people, two of your leading dominos (world and self) have fallen. You cannot rely on the world for happiness, because it doesn't have it. You also cannot rely on self for happiness, because the human creature will drive you to restlessness and unhappiness. What are you going to do now for happiness?

Decide today to not let your life be in vain, but repurpose it to matter and be counted for the cause of Christ.

1. Get to the end of self.
    Quit obsessing with self. You must come to the point of brokenness, defeat, and surrender where you recognize that there is no profit or happiness in living for self. Determine that you exist to serve and glorify God, and not the other way around. Otherwise, you will remain in the boxing ring with God, and the worst chapter of your life has yet to be written.

If your life is you-centric, disappointment is guaranteed. If your personal satisfaction is your highest goal, you will be miserable. But if your life is Christ-centric, there is joy. Stop living for self and start living for Christ.

2. Get equipped.

You must have a working knowledge of the Bible. You are responsible for knowing and articulating the gospel. Learning the Bible takes time and requires serious hard work. A little dab of daily reading will not do you. The Holy Spirit is your best teacher. Pray that He would teach and give you understanding of God's word. Read *James 1:5*. Join a fellowship or study group that teaches the Bible.

3. Get discipled.

Count the cost of discipleship and pray that God would send a spiritually mature person to disciple you. (Discipleship is not a program or a set of lessons where you get a certification of completion at the end. It is a transfer of spiritual maturity from one faithful believer to another, as Paul to Timothy. It includes knowledge and on-the-job training. Read *2Timothy 2:1-7*.)

4. Get engaged.

Your salvation in Jesus Christ includes a call on your life. A pastor asked, "How much do you have to hate people to know that eternal life is possible and not tell them?" Prepare a written testimony of your salvation. This is your conversion story that you can tell in the streets, in group meetings, in emails, in print, or on a blog site. *Romans 10:15b How beautiful are the feet of them that preach the gospel of peace, and bring glad tidings of good things!* A testimony simply consists of three parts: how life was before Jesus, how you met Jesus, and how life is since you received Jesus as Lord and Savior. See the Apostle Paul's example in *Acts 26,* or my testimony in the last chapter of this book.

You may be intimidated to share the gospel with others. That's natural. Your obedience in sharing the gospel is more important than your skill. Simply weave your salvation testimony into regular conversations with friends in a way that is not "in your face." It may be that all you need to say is, "All I know is Jesus saved me. I don't know anything more. Come to church with me and I will introduce you to the people who can explain salvation." The woman at the well in *John 4* did essentially just that. It's a natural outflow from spending time with Jesus. *John 4:28 The woman then left her waterpot, and went her way into the city, and saith to the men, (29) Come, see a man, which told me all things that ever I did: is not this the Christ? (30) Then they went out of the city, and came unto him.* Be sure to live a holy life and make godly decisions so that your testimony is not just empty talk. Over time, your friends will notice your transformation.

In closing, mull over these questions: Can I be happy living for self? Can I be happy not knowing the Bible?

May God open your eyes to see the world for what it really is and recognize the vanity of self serving. May He help you deprogram the world and repurpose your life to matter for Christ and His kingdom.

4 – Vanity of Knowledge

There is a strange problem with knowledge and skills. The more you have, the more miserable you are. Thanks to them, you are in high demand with a full calendar, non-stop conference calls, hundreds of emails a day, text messages, and phones ringing off the hook. Weren't you happier, with more time to enjoy life, when you were less knowledgeable and skillful?

The transformative power of knowledge and its promises for a successful and good life compel us to value learning and endure the painstaking toil of the pursuit of knowledge. We spend a lot of time and money obtaining knowledge and improving academic intelligence. We admire and dignify people with cognitive abilities— the gurus with a string of academic degrees and professional designations behind their names.

Does happiness belong to the learned? Ernest Hemingway wrote, "Happiness in intelligent people is the rarest thing I know." If you are a distinguished person of great intelligence, say hello to loneliness and frustration.

So if knowledge is the chief good and the possession of it is supposed to make one happy, what happens when the excellence of knowledge is all but grief and sorrow? People who trust in knowledge for happiness must rethink their position.

Even so, there may still be those in the self-serving camp who refuse to accept that this world is the vanity of vanities and that happiness is in Jesus Christ only, despite the fact that two of their leading dominos (world and self) have fallen, according to the previous chapter. Now they hide behind the third domino, hoping to find happiness in intellectual prowess. This is not surprising given that our first parents coveted the fruit of the tree of knowledge of good and evil. Therefore, it was appropriate for Solomon to begin his research by learning everything there was to know about human earthly pursuits of happiness.

Ecclesiastes 1:13 And I gave my heart to seek and search out by wisdom concerning all things that are done under heaven: this sore travail hath God given to the sons of man to be exercised therewith.

After proclaiming that all was vanity and substantiating the claim with philosophical proof, Solomon set himself to painstakingly conduct extensive intellectual inquiries and studies into human earthly pursuits of happiness. His mind-blowing mission was to *"seek and search out"*—to discover and to thoroughly learn and examine every matter pertaining to human works of happiness under the sun—*"concerning all things that are done under heaven."* *Proverbs 25:2 It is the glory of God to conceal a thing: but the honour of kings is to search out a matter. (3) The heaven for height, and the earth for depth, and the heart of kings is unsearchable.*

It was a multi-year royal project authorized and led by the king himself, with full priority, funding, and focus. *Ecclesiastes 8:4 Where the word of a king is, there is power: and who may say unto him, What doest thou?* No resources were spared and no stone left unturned. Furthermore, since Jerusalem was the Ivy League center of learning and the rendezvous of academic and political elites (philosophers, intellectuals, scholars, and gurus, as well as successful, affluent, influential, and famous people), Solomon had access to experts from all over the world with whom he conversed and consulted. Imagine the pride and bragging rights of those who met with Solomon. In today's world, these people would take selfies with Solomon and share the photos on social media.

Solomon's learning was guided by wisdom that God gave him in an extraordinary manner. He processed knowledge through wisdom. Verse 13a may be paraphrased as, "I gave my heart to inquire diligently into wisdom concerning all that is done under heaven." This is important, because cognitive prowess without wisdom does not always lead to rational conclusions.

Knowledge didn't come easily to Solomon, even though he gave his heart to learning. The research—all the in-depth fact findings, critical analyses, and examinations—was very burdensome. He associated his quest for knowledge with *"sore travail."* Nevertheless, the king was resolute and fully invested in learning.

The getting of knowledge is by design a *"sore travail."* It is a punishment for the sin of our first parents for coveting the forbidden fruit from the tree of knowledge of good and evil. *Genesis 3:6 And when the woman saw that the tree was good for food, and that it was pleasant to the eyes, and a tree to be desired to make one wise, she took of the fruit thereof, and did eat, and gave also unto her husband with her; and he did eat.* Since then, the affliction (or exercise) of mankind is remaining desire for knowledge, but knowledge doesn't come easily, and learning is tough. As bread is to the body, so is knowledge to the soul—*"all things are full of labour."*

The next five verses can be categorized as follows:

1. The illumination of knowledge – Ecclesiastes 1:14-15.
2. The short-coming of knowledge – Ecclesiastes 1:15.
3. The vexation of knowledge – Ecclesiastes 1:16-17.
4. The vanity of knowledge – Ecclesiastes 1:18.

Ecclesiastes 1:14 I have seen all the works that are done under the sun; and, behold, all is vanity and vexation of spirit. (15) That

which is crooked cannot be made straight: and that which is wanting cannot be numbered.

At the end of his extensive intellectual inquiries and studies, Solomon had considerable empirical proofs to support his thesis. He had considered and weighed all the works of the children of men in their pursuits of happiness *"under the sun"* and learned that:

- *"All is vanity"*
  All self-serving works of happiness *"under the sun"* are vanity or empty. They do not produce true happiness. Solomon was right on the money from the beginning when he proclaimed in his prologue, *"Vanity of vanities, saith the Preacher, vanity of vanities; all is vanity."*

- *"And vexation of spirit"*
  Vexation of spirit is the result of laboring for something that doesn't exist. All the labor is for nothing and it frustrates and distresses the doer.

Among the works of the children of men, Solomon saw the crookedness of their ways, as many prospected for happiness in perverse and illegal ways (such as lies, scandals, and corruptions). This included the numerous imperfect and foolish ways that could never yield happiness.

Through the illumination of knowledge, a learned person sees flaws everywhere. Education teaches the right and proper way of doing things, but in practice, people cut corners because of sin. This happens in every discipline and industry. People even cut corners when it comes to their own happiness by serving self.

The root cause of this problem is the wicked human heart. *Jeremiah 17:9 The heart is deceitful above all things, and desperately wicked: who can know it?* This is a spiritual issue and cannot be fixed by knowledge. Only God can fix the wicked human heart if we let Him.

Solomon thought to reform the people by his vast knowledge—to make straight what he found crooked so that people could find the right path to happiness. As much as he labored to reform the people (which could explain why he referred to himself as a preacher), he discovered a corrupt human nature unfixable by any amount of human wisdom, doomed to a lifetime of hopelessness. This was a bombshell to his hope of obtaining happiness in learning and knowledge.

Humans are by nature corrupt, and no secular or social means can reform them. They are like a car going down the road with a broken tie rod unable to keep a straight line. The human sin nature predisposes individuals to walk in the course of vanity—serving self and seeking happiness in worldly things that do not satisfy. Sinners can only be reformed and transformed into new creatures by the Spirit of God. Our job is to pray for them and share the gospel of Christ in humility and love. Only God can make straight (holy) that which is crooked (sinful). *Isaiah 42:16 And I will bring the blind by a way that they knew not; I will lead them in paths that they have not known: I will make darkness light before them, and crooked things straight. These things will I do unto them, and not forsake them.* Read *Ecclesiastes 7:13, Luke 3:4-6.*

Ecclesiastes 1:16 I communed with mine own heart, saying, Lo, I am come to great estate, and have gotten more wisdom than all they that have been before me in Jerusalem: yea, my heart had great experience of wisdom and knowledge. (17) And I gave my heart to know wisdom, and to know madness and folly: I perceived that this also is vexation of spirit. (18) For in much wisdom is much grief: and he that increaseth knowledge increaseth sorrow.

Disappointed with his inability to mend and reform human sinfulness, Solomon pathetically recounted his attainments. He noted that he had arrived at the highest pitch of knowledge—*"come to great estate,"* and was more skillful in applying knowledge than all his predecessors in Jerusalem. The word *"yea"* underscores his great experience, in that truly, he mastered the application of knowledge. *1Kings 4:29 And God gave Solomon wisdom and understanding exceeding much, and largeness of heart, even as the sand that is on the sea shore. (30) And Solomon's wisdom excelled the wisdom of all the children of the east country, and all the wisdom of Egypt. (31) For he was wiser than all men; than Ethan the Ezrahite, and Heman, and Chalcol, and Darda, the sons of Mahol: and his fame was in all nations round about. (32) And he spake three thousand proverbs: and his songs were a thousand and five. (33) And he spake of trees, from the cedar tree that is in Lebanon even unto the hyssop that springeth out of the wall: he spake also of beasts, and of fowl, and of creeping things, and of fishes.*

Solomon's experience of wisdom and madness and folly was not superficial. In *Ecclesiastes 7:25*, he said, *"I applied mine heart to know, and to search, and to seek out wisdom, and the reason of things, and to know the wickedness of folly, even of foolishness and madness."* He was resolved to know not only about things, but the reason of things. He personally experienced the inner workings of wisdom and madness and folly. (The word *"know"* in the Bible denotes relationship. For example, *Genesis 4:1a Adam knew Eve his wife; and she conceived, and bare Cain.* Also, to know God is not to have facts about Him, but to be in relationship with Him.) With intimate knowledge of both the yin and the yang, he was able to compare and contrast the goodness of wisdom with the foolishness of folly.

In the end, Solomon realized that knowledge was a *"vexation of spirit."* He discovered that his vast skill and experience gave him a lot of grief. And as he became more knowledgeable, he increased in sorrow instead of happiness. He received no satisfaction. The more he learned, the more he realized how messed up and hopeless people were, causing him more sorrow.

This is not hard to understand. Imagine you are the world's top nutritionist. You have years of painstaking research and learning under your belt. You know how the body uses nutrients and the relationship between diet, health, and disease. However, you see people everywhere loving and eating processed junk foods, and you are powerless to change their behavior. Your knowledge and wisdom frustrate rather than satisfy you. The more you learn about nutrition and what people should eat, the more you discover what they shouldn't eat, and become more frustrated. You go home every day mad at the companies that produce junk food.

While knowledge unlocks worldly success, there is no happiness in it, regardless of the discipline. Every discipline teaches the right way, but the world is full of imperfections and people who make bad decisions—*"That which is crooked cannot be made straight: and that which is wanting cannot be numbered."* The more you learn what's right, the more you see what's wrong and opportunities for improvement, resulting in dissatisfaction. If you are banking on knowledge for happiness, you are rerunning an experiment that has been proven to disappoint. In my business, I interact with many experts who ooze knowledge. They have a proud "don't you dare challenge me" attitude and are ever ready to present and debate issues. Yet behind the façade is nothing but misery and unhappiness. One of my coworkers, an MIT graduate, committed suicide. He had much worldly success by his knowledge, but failed to secure the happiness he was looking for.

Final Thoughts

We learn that our felicity rests not in learning or intellectual capital—*"Let not the wise man glory in his wisdom."* While knowledge is useful to individuals (*Proverbs 9:12*), it falls short of delivering happiness.

The acquisition of knowledge is labor intensive, yet we should not be without knowledge. We should obtain the vital degrees and professional certifications to make a better living. However, if knowledge is all that makes and defines us, life has little satisfaction.

The celestial knowledge of the word of God is enlightening, satisfying, and profitable, as it is capable of producing eternal results. *2Timothy 3:15 And that from a child thou hast known the holy scriptures, which are able to make thee wise unto salvation through faith which is in Christ Jesus. (16) All scripture is given by inspiration of God, and is profitable for doctrine, for reproof, for correction, for instruction in righteousness: (17) That the man of God may be perfect, throughly furnished unto all good works.* Read *Psalms 19:7-14.*

Learning the Bible is hard, but life is harder not knowing and living the Bible. Many people who read the Bible either get tired quickly or don't get beyond the stories. They don't understand what it means to learn the Bible and consequently, the most important book in their life becomes irrelevant. It takes serious effort and time to learn the Bible, as nothing worthwhile comes easily, and nothing great can be achieved quickly and effortlessly. It is precept upon precept, line upon line, here a little, and there a little, according to *Isaiah 28:9-10.* Yet we should not be discouraged from the pursuit of holy knowledge. It gives us sound doctrines so that we are not deceived by people who sow heresies, offer worldly fixes to spiritual problems, and tickle our ears with fluffy feel-good messages. *Ephesians 4:14 That we henceforth be no more children, tossed to and fro, and carried about with every wind of doctrine, by the sleight of men, and cunning craftiness, whereby they lie in wait to deceive.*

We need to learn God's word to fix life issues and live a fulfilled life. Casual Bible reading as a chapter a day to keep the devil away does not work. We need to acquire a working knowledge of the Bible by prayerfully, obediently, and diligently studying it, not for the sake of gathering more facts, because knowledge puffs us up, but that we may live the truth and please God. *2Timothy 2:15 Study to shew thyself approved unto God, a workman that needeth not to be ashamed, rightly dividing the word of truth.* Learning how to study the Bible is a necessary life skill for Christians.

For example, did you know the entire Bible is written <u>for</u> you, but not all the Bible is written <u>to</u> you? Read *1Corinthians 10:1-11*. The Bible addresses three groups of people—Jews, Gentiles, and the Church (Christians) across multiple dispensational periods. Failure to rightly divide the word of truth results in many bad teachings and the rise of religious cults. Righteousness by good works, baptismal regeneration, and losing salvation are examples of misapplication of scriptures. Tragically, millions of people are still going to hell through the "Christianity" portal, because they do not know scriptures, choosing to trust in people or religious banners.

The bottom line is that if we don't know the Bible, we don't know what God says, and therefore our hope may be misplaced, because people place their hopes based on what they know. If we invest in the word of God, a few years from now, we will not recognize the persons we are today. I recommend the following resources that will help you learn the Bible.

- #Wordstrong http://wordstrong.me/keys-of-bible-study
- Searching for Truth: https://goo.gl/l958P3
- Reality Living: https://goo.gl/msFBhV. Check out the "Basic principles of Bible study" in Appendix I, and "How to find a good church" in Appendix II.

- Midtown Baptist Temple http://mbtkc.org/sermons has a treasure trove of Bible study materials.

Decide today to live a life that matters by learning, living, and sharing God's word through evangelism and discipleship. *Proverbs 11:30 The fruit of the righteous is a tree of life; and he that winneth souls is wise.* May God richly bless you with His knowledge, and may your light shine brighter with each passing day.

5 – Vanity of Worldly Pleasures and Possessions

I n exchange for living large—playing like a king, eating like a king, and living like a king everyday of your life—you promise to never again worship God, read the Bible, attend church, and pray in Jesus' name. Deal?

Featured herein are the sensual pleasures of entertainment, feasting, and owning—the things that the children of the world are fond of, flattering themselves with expectations of happiness. Do you think they will be happy?

Ecclesiastes 2:1 I said in mine heart, Go to now, I will prove thee with mirth, therefore enjoy pleasure: and, behold, this also is vanity. (2) I said of laughter, It is mad: and of mirth, What doeth it?

Since the noble pleasures of learning and knowledge, believed to make a person wise, failed to yield happiness, there was nothing else for Solomon to explore on the wise side of the fence, so he knocked on the other side—sensual pleasures. He approved and released himself to be the test subject of worldly pleasures and possessions.

The phrase *"Go to now"* means a departure from God. God did not ask Solomon to do this, but allowed it to happen. Solomon said "I" 20 times in the first 11 verses of *Ecclesiastes 2*. God blessed Solomon with grace and everything he needed to experiment with in order to discover happiness. Solomon was able to experience the full spectrum from wisdom to madness and folly. He got to live wisely and foolishly, and was able to recover from foolishness, because his wisdom remained with him, according to *Ecclesiastes 2:9*.

Notice that disobedience begins in the heart—*"I said in mine heart."* The reason we find ourselves on the foolish side of the fence is because somewhere along the line, our hearts said, *"Go to now;"* go and taste worldly pleasures. We make a conscientious decision to depart from God, stop serving Him, and focus on self to live an ostentatious and decadent lifestyle.

Departing from God to experience madness and folly is not something we want to replicate. We are not Solomon and will soon find ourselves drowning in the deep end. It is like the disclaimer before a dangerous TV scene—"Don't try this at home. It is for highly trained professionals only."

Solomon first tempted himself with mirth because *"the heart of fools is in the house of mirth,"* according to *Ecclesiastes 7:4b*. Mirth is the amusement of senses, especially as expressed in laughter. It comes in various forms from innocent to dirty—anything that puts people in a jovial mood.

Late night television comedies are a form of mirth. Not much effort is needed from the audience other than to be comfortably seated and entertained. This is a stark contrast to the noble pleasure of learning, which is laborious. So if extreme learning does not make one happy, perhaps good hearty laughs will? Is laughter really the best medicine?

The children of the world love the pleasure of entertainment, so it is not surprising that mirth leads the way. They love places like Las Vegas where they can be entertained and act stupid. *Proverbs 15:21a* says, *"Folly is joy to him that is destitute of wisdom."*

The logic is to be dumb and happy, and is simply this: "I am tired of being unhappy. I am going to manufacture happiness through mirth." Unfortunately, this logic doesn't fly. *Isaiah 50:11 Behold, all ye that kindle a fire, that compass yourselves about with sparks: walk in the light of your fire, and in the sparks that ye have kindled. This shall ye have of mine hand; ye shall lie down in sorrow.* Anything that people manufacture for happiness will disappoint.

That said, mirth is not necessarily sinful. Innocent mirth used moderately helps soften the stress of life. However, too much mirth may cause people to be hysterical and act insanely—*"I said of laughter, It is mad."* Notice how quickly—in the same sentence— Solomon dismissed the ability of mirth to deliver solid and substantial happiness. The river object lesson in *Ecclesiastes 1:7a* already warned us of this, *"All the rivers run into the sea; yet the sea is not full."* All the rivers of worldly pleasure will never be able to make one happy.

Mirth fails to erase depression and the pain of emptiness. *Proverbs 14:13 Even in laughter the heart is sorrowful; and the end of that mirth is heaviness.* How many high-profile suicides have shocked the nation because the stars looked so happy on the outside, but inside they were ravaged with depression?

Ecclesiastes 2:3 I sought in mine heart to give myself unto wine, yet acquainting mine heart with wisdom; and to lay hold on folly, till I might see what was that good for the sons of men, which they should do under the heaven all the days of their life.

Feasting is also a form of mirth. *Ecclesiastes 8:15a Then I commended mirth, because a man hath no better thing under the sun, than to eat, and to drink, and to be merry. Ecclesiastes 10:19a A feast is made for laughter, and wine maketh merry.*

The word *"wine"* in *Ecclesiastes 2:3* refers to feasts of fine food and drinks. On trial here is the pleasure of feasting involving good food and company. How would you like to be able to satisfy your palate every day with lavish Michelin-starred, mouth-watering gastronomic feasts that are fit for a king while enjoying good conversation and laughter with friends? Would you be happy?

People in my Asian culture tend to love showing off their social status by savoring 10-course meals featuring such expensive gourmet items as shark fin and abalone. Here we have a real king who ate like a king. *1Kings 4:22 And Solomon's provision for one day was thirty measures of fine flour, and threescore measures of meal, (23) Ten fat oxen, and twenty oxen out of the pastures, and an hundred sheep, beside harts, and roebucks, and fallowdeer, and fatted fowl.* Obviously Solomon couldn't eat that portion all by himself in one day. It was for his household and friends.

Solomon gave himself to immoderate indulgence—*"I sought in mine heart to give myself unto wine,"* to make a trial of what the children of the world deem as happiness. But Solomon wasn't about to binge or be a stupid drunk, because then he would lose command of his cognitive faculties and become an incompetent judge. He was guided by wisdom in his research of happiness—*"yet acquainting mine heart with wisdom,"* as he did in *Ecclesiastes 1:13* when he gave himself to learning. His experiment was under the check and control of wisdom to demonstrate the known truth, which is *"all is vanity."* In other words, Solomon managed himself wisely in his indulgence in fine foods and drinks among friends.

Besides *"wine,"* Solomon also indulged in other foolish things that the children of the world deem to bring happiness, some of which he enumerated in the next five verses. Solomon put himself through these experiments to find out what was good for self-serving people to do during their brief existence in this world—*"till I might see what was that good for the sons of men, which they should do under the heaven all the days of their life."*

Ecclesiastes 2:4 I made me great works; I builded me houses; I planted me vineyards: (5) I made me gardens and orchards, and I planted trees in them of all kind of fruits: (6) I made me pools of water, to water therewith the wood that bringeth forth trees:

Solomon adorned his debauchery with material pleasures. He built costly palaces and playgrounds and collected expensive one-of-a-kind toys. He obtained great riches and was served by an entourage of servants.

In terms of luxury living spaces, one of Solomon's palaces took 13 years to construct. Read about it in *1Kings 7:1-12*, and notice that *"costly stones"* is mentioned three times. His royal seat in the porch of judgment was a great ivory throne overlaid with fine gold. All of Solomon's drinking vessels were of pure gold. Read *1Kings 10:18-21*.

What is a palace without an enchanting idyllic royal garden? Solomon's palatial playgrounds and outdoor enjoyments included fertile and sublime vineyards, gardens, and orchards with floras, faunas, and practical water features that were charming and captivating. He had vineyards in Engedi and Baalhamon, according to *The Song of Solomon 1:14, 8:11*. Solomon loved to relax, rejuvenate, and connect with nature in his vineyards while enjoying the tranquil retreat with the sweet harmonious sound of nature in his blossoming fragrant gardens. *The Song of Solomon 7:12 Let us get up early to the vineyards; let us see if the vine flourish, whether the tender grape appear, and the pomegranates bud forth: there will I give thee my loves.*

Surely, if happiness is in owning luxury real estate, Solomon would have been the wisest, richest, and happiest man in the world. But this too is vanity, according to *Ecclesiastes 2:11*.

Just for fun, compare Solomon's man-engineered Eden with Adam's Eden. In Adam's Eden, God did everything for him. *Genesis 2:8 And the LORD God planted a garden eastward in Eden; and there he put the man whom he had formed. (9) And out of the ground made the LORD God to grow every tree that is pleasant to the sight, and good for food; the tree of life also in the midst of the garden, and the tree of knowledge of good and evil. (10) And a river went out of Eden to water the garden; and from thence it was parted, and became into four heads.*

Ecclesiastes 2:7 I got me servants and maidens, and had servants born in my house; also I had great possessions of great and small cattle above all that were in Jerusalem before me: (8) I gathered me also silver and gold, and the peculiar treasure of kings and of the provinces: I gat me men singers and women singers, and the delights of the sons of men, as musical instruments, and that of all sorts.

What is a king without a retinue of servants to wait on him hand and foot? Solomon bought many servants, both men and women. The number of house-born servants also multiplied. (The servants' children who were born in Solomon's house were known as "house-born," and they belonged to him.) These servants weren't treated like slaves. They were happy servants. *1Kings 10:4 And when the queen of Sheba had seen all Solomon's wisdom, and the house that he had built, (5) And the meat of his table, and the sitting of his servants, and the attendance of his ministers, and their apparel, and his cupbearers, and his ascent by which he went up unto the house of the LORD; there was no more spirit in her. (6) And she said to the king, It was a true report that I heard in mine own land of thy acts and of thy wisdom. (7) Howbeit I believed not the words, until I came, and mine eyes had seen it: and, behold, the half was not told me: thy wisdom and prosperity exceedeth the fame which I heard. (8) Happy are thy men, happy are these thy servants, which stand continually before thee, and that hear thy wisdom.*

With the number of servants in the thousands, Solomon didn't have to lift a finger his whole life. The well-trained staff ensured that no detail went unnoticed, meticulously attending to every nuance for his comfort. Surely, if this uber-luxe, pampered lifestyle brought happiness, Solomon would have announced it rather than denounce it.

Affordability was not in Solomon's vocabulary. His cattle increased to a record number in Jerusalem. The word *"cattle"* is generic for such livestock as oxen, cows, horses, asses, camels, mules, sheep, and goats. Besides being used in religious sacrificial rites, agriculture, and transportation, they were a form of currency used in trade and for gifts. In biblical times, a man's wealth was measured by the number of livestock he owned. *Genesis 24:35 And the LORD hath blessed my master* (Abraham) *greatly; and he is become great: and he hath given him flocks, and herds, and silver, and gold, and menservants, and maidservants, and camels, and asses.*

Solomon amassed silver and gold in great quantities. *1Kings 10:14 Now the weight of gold that came to Solomon in one year was six hundred threescore and six talents of gold.* That was about 20 metric tons of gold in one year. (Common people may have owned a few ounces of gold coins, while the rich may have owned a few kilos of gold bars. But Solomon's gold was measured in tons.) So great was the quantity of the gold that nobody cared to weigh the silver, for it was as abundant and as common as stones. *1Kings 10:27a And the king made silver to be in Jerusalem as stones.*

Solomon had a collection of rare, exquisite treasures from royalties and provinces. *1Kings 4:21 And Solomon reigned over all kingdoms from the river unto the land of the Philistines, and unto the border of Egypt: they brought presents, and served Solomon all the days of his life.* There is nothing new under the sun. Today people collect exotic cars, paintings, gems, sports memorabilia, etc.

Solomon crowned his immense riches with music. His scrumptious banquets and social events were splendid and lively with professional singers with impeccable voices and musicians capable of playing all sorts of musical instruments, which gave great pleasure to all. Live concerts, open bars, and good food—life was good! *Isaiah 5:12 And the harp, and the viol, the tabret, and pipe, and wine, are in their feasts: but they regard not the work of the LORD, neither consider the operation of his hands.*

Ecclesiastes 2:9 So I was great, and increased more than all that were before me in Jerusalem: also my wisdom remained with me. (10) And whatsoever mine eyes desired I kept not from them, I withheld not my heart from any joy; for my heart rejoiced in all my labour: and this was my portion of all my labour.

Solomon was magnified in his possessions and in his amplified debauchery and extravagance. His possessions exceeded all that were before him in Jerusalem. *1Kings 10:23 So king Solomon exceeded all the kings of the earth for riches and for wisdom.* And his wisdom stood by him to help him be a better judge while he took full liberty, indulging in worldly pleasures. He was the crème de la crème, the most enviable person in the world as the poster child of happiness—rich, wise, and powerful. If he was alive today, his face would be on every billboard and advertisement.

In the course of procuring pleasure, he gave in to unbridled lust of the eyes and of the flesh. Imagine the gratifications from such sinful sybaritic indulgences. His heart was delighted to taste the pleasures from his accomplishments. *1Kings 11:3a And he had seven hundred wives, princesses, and three hundred concubines.*

Solomon referred to his accomplishments as the *"portion of all my labor,"* for which he worked hard. He made other royals jealous. The queen of Sheba was astonished when she saw his magnificent kingdom and the honor of his excellent majesty, according to *1Kings 10:4-5.* This portion is what the children of the world dream of in life—exclusive world-class luxuries and pleasures in grandeur. Many people would settle for a fraction of what he had. The American dream is a pathetic comparison.

Ecclesiastes 2:11 Then I looked on all the works that my hands had wrought, and on the labour that I had laboured to do: and, behold, all was vanity and vexation of spirit, and there was no profit under the sun.

After years of walking in the flesh, Solomon looked and considered all the works that he had ever laid his hands on and the wearisome labor he had undertaken and concluded that:

- *"All was vanity and vexation of spirit"* – With such advantages and opportunities beyond the reach of others, and with such incredible resources at his command, if true happiness could have been found, Solomon would have found it. But all he found was emptiness.

  Worldly pleasures gratify the outward flesh, but they vex the spirit, which is the energy of life. A lot of emphasis is put on physical health with little attention paid to spiritual harmony. Mark the unrepentant people who give in to sinful worldly pleasures. They have health, mental, and emotional issues. *Galatians 6:7 Be not deceived; God is not mocked: for whatsoever a man soweth, that shall he also reap. (8) For he that soweth to his flesh shall of the flesh reap corruption; but he that soweth to the Spirit shall of the Spirit reap life everlasting.*

- *"There was no profit under the sun"* – Take a look at all the things that you have manufactured for happiness and the sparks and fire that you have kindled (*Isaiah 50:11*) to make you happy, and name one that yields happiness. Since Solomon's grand version of debauchery didn't deliver happiness, what makes you think your miniature version will? Is it time for you to reset your affection to things above? *Colossians 3:1 If ye then be risen with Christ, seek those things which are above, where Christ sitteth on the right hand of God. (2) Set your affection on things above, not on things on the earth. (3) For ye are dead, and your life is hid with Christ in God.*

Consider this diary note of an unrepentant person who remains on the path of debauchery: "Personally, I find the quick fix exciting, but since it's fleeting, it doesn't last. Similar to the effects of booze, I'm happy and intoxicated, feeling good, but the next day, well, not so much. I guess I want something more... something of substance, but without the 24/7 clingy vibe of having to answer to someone every minute." This person represents millions of people who are on the same sinful path of vanity. It's a meat market out there. The world says, "No strings attached." God says, "There is a chain called sin. It will cause you all kinds of problems, and it will kill you." Be forewarned by this saying, "Sin will take you farther than you want to go, keep you longer than you want to stay, and cost you more than you want to pay."

A voluptuous and lascivious lifestyle is not cheap to acquire and maintain. Nowadays many people are in the devil's den seeking happiness in pornography, adultery, and fornication. The lusts of sensuality are not financially or spiritually sustainable. *Proverbs 21:17a says, "He that loveth pleasure shall be a poor man."* 1Peter

2:11b says, *"Abstain from fleshly lusts, which war against the soul."* This invalidates the Hedonism and Epicureanism philosophies, which argue that pleasure is the primary or most important intrinsic good. An ancient Egyptian poem rooted in Hedonism says:

> Let thy desire flourish,
> In order to let thy heart forget the beatifications for thee.
> Follow thy desire, as long as thou shalt live.
> Put myrrh upon thy head and clothing of fine linen upon thee,
> Being anointed with genuine marvels of the gods' property.
> Set an increase to thy good things;
> Let not thy heart flag.
> Follow thy desire and thy good.
> Fulfill thy needs upon earth, after the command of thy heart,
> Until there come for thee that day of mourning.

The response to the above poem is *Proverbs 28:26, "He that trusteth in his own heart is a fool: but whoso walketh wisely, he shall be delivered."* Also according to *Jeremiah 17:9, "The heart is deceitful above all things, and desperately wicked: who can know it?"*

Pause to ponder what good is a self-serving life. *Job 21:14 Therefore they say unto God, Depart from us; for we desire not the knowledge of thy ways. (15) What is the Almighty, that we should serve him? and what profit should we have, if we pray unto him?* Sadly, too many people are perfectly content with vanity. They are proud of their material accumulations and see absolutely no need for Christ or to serve Him. *Revelation 3:17 Because thou sayest, I am rich, and increased with goods, and have need of nothing; and knowest not that thou art wretched, and miserable, and poor, and blind, and naked.*

May God give you the wisdom to recognize the gimmicks of the world and conclude that self-serving is vanity and that you would be better off serving Him.

The following chart summarizes the trials:

Trial	Gratification	Lifestyle	Logic
Mirth	Sensual pleasure in entertainment	Play like a king	Be dumb and happy. "Laughter is the best medicine," so I want to be entertained and laugh my way out of depression and the pain of emptiness.
"Wine" – Fine foods and drinks	Sensual pleasure in feasting	Eat like a king	Be fat and happy. I want to feast my way out of depression and the pain of emptiness.
Worldly possessions	Sensual pleasure in owning	Live like a king	Be rich and happy. Things will get me out of depression and the pain of emptiness.

Final Thoughts

We learn that our felicity rests not in sensual delights or material possessions. The lifestyles of "play like a king," "eat like a king," and "live like a king" fail to yield happiness. What initially seems to be pure elation and enjoyment ends up being vanity and vexation of spirit, and we remain unsatisfied.

Stop imitating the ungodly in trying to extract as much pleasure out of life as possible, serving God with leftovers. Don't fall for the world's deceptions that lead to derailment and entrapment.

Like the carnivorous Pitcher plants that lure unsuspected insects with their looks and sweet nectar, the world tantalizes us with easy, blissful, splashy, extravagant, and sinful lifestyles that appeal to the sensual flesh, and many people fall for them. (It is helpful to remember that the devil offered the world to Jesus, but He chose the cross instead. Read *Matthew 4:8-10.*) Worldly focused people covet the lifestyles, chase vain happiness, and spend their most productive years on themselves, missing the opportunity to serve God.

Those of us who have fallen countless times before should know by now that we are only inches away from the slippery slopes leading to hurtful traps and that our obedience to the word of God is the only thing that anchors and keeps us from falling again.

What makes us happy is the satisfaction of living the truth, sowing the seeds of truth, harvesting souls for the kingdom of God, and discipling young believers and seeing their lives transformed. We are satisfied when we are conformed to the image of Christ. *Psalms 17:15 As for me, I will behold thy face in righteousness: I shall be satisfied, when I awake, with thy likeness.*

Below are some practical things that you may be able to do to live a life that matters. Know the things that are near and dear to God's heart. He wants to set up a kingdom on earth in which His Son, Jesus Christ, reigns as King of Kings and Lord of Lords. *Isaiah 9:6 For unto us a child is born, unto us a son is given: and the government shall be upon his shoulder: and his name shall be called Wonderful, Counsellor, The mighty God, The everlasting Father, The Prince of Peace. (7) Of the increase of his government and peace there shall be no end, upon the throne of David, and upon his kingdom, to order it, and to establish it with judgment and with justice from henceforth even for ever. The zeal of the LORD of hosts will perform this.*

- Have the same kingdom mindset, focusing your life on the Father's business. How are you improving God's economy with your life and the resources that He gave you?

- Pray for the advancement of His kingdom in your life. *Luke 11:2 And he said unto them, When ye pray, say, Our Father which art in heaven, Hallowed be thy name. Thy kingdom come. Thy will be done, as in heaven, so in earth.*

- Repent of besetting sins. *Hebrews 12:1 Wherefore seeing we also are compassed about with so great a cloud of witnesses, let us lay aside every weight, and the sin which doth so easily beset us, and let us run with patience the race that is set before us, (2) Looking unto Jesus the author and finisher of our faith; who for the joy that was set before him endured the cross, despising the shame, and is set down at the right hand of the throne of God.* Now, this does not mean you go outside and stare at the sky. Jesus' face is the word of God. *1John 1:1 That which was from the beginning, which we have heard, which we have seen with our eyes, which we have looked upon, and our hands have handled, of the Word of life.* "Turn your eyes upon Jesus, Look full in His wonderful face, And the things of earth will grow strangely dim, In the light of His glory and grace."—Chorus from "Turn Your Eyes upon Jesus" hymn by Helen H. Lemmel.

If you are living your life in pursuit of the sins of the flesh, something is fundamentally wrong, and I would encourage you to check your salvation. Perhaps all you have is a religion or a religious experience and not a right relationship with God through Jesus Christ. *1John 3:9 Whosoever is born of God doth not commit sin; for his seed remaineth in him: and he cannot sin, because he is born of God.* Those who are truly born again cannot dwell in sin. Consider Moses, "*Choosing rather to suffer affliction with the people of God, than to enjoy the pleasures of sin for a season.*" (Hebrews 11:25)

- Take care of your financial debts and work toward being debt free. Many good-hearted Christians who wish to do kingdom work are frustrated by financial problems. Are you racking up more debt for stuff that does not satisfy? *Isaiah 55:2 Wherefore do ye spend money for that which is not bread? and your labour for that which satisfieth not? hearken diligently unto me, and eat ye that which is good, and let your soul delight itself in fatness. (3) Incline your ear, and come unto me: hear, and your soul shall live; and I will make an everlasting covenant with you, even the sure mercies of David.* Imagine the additional ministry opportunities you can participate in if you are debt free.

- Let go of the world. Write it off, and set your affections on things above. Loving the world over God is committing spiritual fornication. Be content with what you have. *Hebrews 13:5 Let your conversation be without covetousness; and be content with such things as ye have: for he hath said, I will never leave thee, nor forsake thee.* Read *Philippians 4:11-13.* Practice godly contentment. Some people resign to grudging contentment because they can't afford the things they want. Godly contentment is the rejection of the world for the pursuit of holy living that yields the fruit of the Spirit. Read *1Timothy 6:6-12.* It is only possible when Jesus is Lord and affections are set on the things above. *Psalms 23:1 The LORD is my shepherd; I shall not want.*

Decide today to take up your cross, crucifying your plans and desires, and live for Christ. *Matthew 16:24 Then said Jesus unto his disciples, If any man will come after me, let him deny himself, and take up his cross, and follow me.* May God give you wisdom and help you to overcome the world.

Consider the following two verses of the hymn, "I'd rather have Jesus" by Rhea F. Miller.

> I'd rather have Jesus than silver or gold,
> I'd rather be His than have riches untold;
> I'd rather have Jesus than houses or land,
> Yes, I'd rather be led by His nail-pierced hand.
>
> Chorus:
> Than to be the king of a vast domain
> And be held in sin's dread sway
> I'd rather have Jesus than anything
> This world affords today.
>
> I'd rather have Jesus than worldly applause,
> I'd rather be faithful to His dear cause;
> I'd rather have Jesus than worldwide fame,
> I'd rather be true to His holy name.

6 – Vanity of Worldly Success

One event causes successful professionals to hate their lives and accomplishments and to despair of all their works. This too will happen to you if you are the professional described in this chapter.

Featured herein are two extreme individuals: a profound professional who spends his entire life on achieving worldly success and a fool who wastes his life in frenzied folly. It shows that if life is limited to this world only, the professional, who may be a successful executive of a Fortune 500 company with a huge estate, is no better than the fool.

Ecclesiastes 2:12 And I turned myself to behold wisdom, and madness, and folly: for what can the man do that cometh after the king? even that which hath been already done.

Solomon tried extreme learning in *Ecclesiastes 1:13-18* and found that knowledge and wisdom yielded grief and sorrow instead of happiness. He then tried extreme folly in *Ecclesiastes 2:1-11* and also found no happiness.

His new understanding was utterly depressing. There is no happiness on either side of the fence. It is reasonable to expect no happiness from the foolish side, but if the wise side also comes up empty, then what's in it for those who invest in learning and building a successful life for themselves under the sun? These people are highly educated and are outstanding citizens with good careers. They live in nice neighborhoods, and their children go to good schools. They also contribute much to society.

Is it preposterous that happiness eludes self-serving professionals? How many professionals do you know who have committed suicide because they weren't happy?

Yikes! The wise and the fools are no different when they live for self under the sun.

Solomon was careful not to miss anything in his research. He wanted to be sure that he went far enough in every way so that no one could challenge his findings. Indeed, everything he did was extreme—extreme learning, extreme entertainment, extreme feasting, extreme living, extreme debauchery, etc. If such extreme measures failed to secure happiness, all lesser versions have no hope.

To be sure, he double checked his works and was certain that no one could improve upon what he had done. We have with us the "Solomon guarantee."

Ecclesiastes 2:13 Then I saw that wisdom excelleth folly, as far as light excelleth darkness. (14) The wise man's eyes are in his head; but the fool walketh in darkness: and I myself perceived also that one event happeneth to them all.

As pursuit of success takes time and hard work, successful people deserve to be recognized and rewarded for their achievements. *Proverbs 12:8 A man shall be commended according to his wisdom: but he that is of a perverse heart shall be despised.* High achievers are an important and valuable part of society. Many are kind and generous with their time and wealth. Their traits and habits inspire many wannabes.

Even though self-serving professionals and fools share a common fate concerning happiness, wisdom (skills acquired through knowledge and experience) is far more profitable to an individual than is folly. (The word "*excelleth*" is also translated as "profit.") Wisdom excels folly in the same way that light excels darkness. The difference is night and day. This is not rocket science. Learned and skillful people have a better life than fools. Wisdom helps them to make sound decisions leading to a good and safe life.

The eyes, or focus, of smart people is in the proper place. The light of knowledge helps them navigate their courses. Fools however, walk in darkness, because they hate knowledge, according to *Proverbs 1:22b*. They do not apply themselves to acquiring knowledge through studying, but instead give themselves to the pleasures of folly. Without the light of knowledge, fools grope and stumble in their way, making costly bad life decisions, and crashing and burning. Their eyes might as well not be in their heads, like some blind cave fish, because they choose to walk in darkness. Eyes need light to function and are useless in absolute darkness. Read *Psalms 107:10-12*.

The application here is that one must invest in knowledge to live a better and more enjoyable life, both physical and spiritual.

Are the eyes of your understanding getting spiritual light from the Bible? Otherwise, you might as well not have spiritual eyes. *Ephesians 1:17 That the God of our Lord Jesus Christ, the Father of glory, may give unto you the spirit of wisdom and revelation in the knowledge of him: (18) The eyes of your understanding being enlightened; that ye may know what is the hope of his calling, and what the riches of the glory of his inheritance in the saints, (19) And what is the exceeding greatness of his power to us-ward who believe, according to the working of his mighty power.*

While the knowledge and skills of professionals set them apart from fools, how quickly they meet again, because one event—death—brings them together. The successes of professionals are not able to deliver them from death.

The perception of inevitable death is the trigger point that sends smart and successful people spiraling down to despair. Everyone has a non-cancellable appointment with God; being dead is the least problem. *Hebrews 9:27 And as it is appointed unto men once to die, but after this the judgment.* The Bible also talks about a second death for those who reject Jesus Christ as Lord and Savior, according to *Revelation 20:11-15*. There is a saying that if you are born once, you will die twice (physical and spiritual deaths), but if you are born twice, you only die once (physical death).

Ecclesiastes 2:15 Then said I in my heart, As it happeneth to the fool, so it happeneth even to me; and why was I then more wise? Then I said in my heart, that this also is vanity.

Death does not discriminate. It hits the wise as it hits fools. When both the professional and the fool lay in their caskets, is there a difference in their end state? Then what's the point of enduring the pain of learning, working hard to differentiate oneself, and building a successful life in this world when death levels and sweeps away all distinctions? Is this not vanity?

This is the onset of frustration, which spirals down to hopelessness for successful self-serving people, as shown in verses 17–23 below. Many choose to kill themselves.

Ecclesiastes 2:16 For there is no remembrance of the wise more than of the fool for ever; seeing that which now is in the days to come shall all be forgotten. And how dieth the wise man? as the fool.

There is no consolation to smart, diligent, and successful people who might have hoped to be at least remembered for their good works and contributions to the world. Case in point, how many people remember the name and legacy of the sugar magnate who owned the sugar mills in the U.S. Virgin Islands in 1780, less than three centuries ago? Didn't he leave this world in better shape than he found it?

Consider numerous other successful business people, famous athletes, singers, and movie stars whose names are now in oblivion. (In contrast, *"the righteous shall be in everlasting remembrance,"* according to *Psalms 112:6b*; not in this world, but in the world to come.) Billionaires nowadays are trying to keep their legacy alive with artistic and architectural immortality. They spend a lot of money getting their names on buildings, leaving a lasting mark on their cities. This too is vanity as everything will decay and be replaced. (The Sears Tower in Chicago was once the tallest in the world. It was renamed The Willis Tower in 2009. Less than 10 years after the name change, many Millennials don't even recognize the Sears Tower name.)

Think you can leave a lasting impression on this world? Go to the beach and make your footprints in the sand. What happens to those prints when the waves wash over them? It will be as if you had never been there. Others will make their prints on top of yours. You may be the bomb right now, but when you die, it will be as if you had never lived.

Imagine the dead body of a successful corporate executive laying next to the corpse of a homeless drug addict in a funeral home. Worldly success cannot prevent the executive from being reduced to the same condition as the fool. Both stink and become worm food. *Job 21:26 They shall lie down alike in the dust, and the worms shall cover them.*

What advantage does the professional have over the fool? They both wasted their lives. The executive wasted his talents and life in chasing after worldly success, while the drug addict wasted his life in folly. Their friends may say, "He died doing the thing he loved," but the cold, harsh reality is that they both died the fool's death.

To make this more striking, put a dead dog between them. Is there any difference in their end state if there is no hereafter? Are those two better than the dead dog? *Ecclesiastes 3:18 I said in mine heart concerning the estate of the sons of men, that God might manifest them, and that they might see that they themselves are beasts.* From God's perspective, the dead dog was more faithful and serviceable to its master than the two fools who served the wrong master. The dog gave its master joy. (A fool is not one with a low IQ or inability to think, but is one who refuses to acknowledge the truth and submit to God.)

People like to think that the world is a better place because of them. How ironic it is for people who live for self to think that? This is nothing more than unrepentant rebellion and continual refusal to acknowledge and serve God.

Below is a recap on how the self-serving wise and fools are alike:

- Both share a common fate concerning happiness.
- Death happens to both.
- Both have the same end state.
- Both will eventually be forgotten.

If worldly success is all that defines you, the above is your deal under the sun.

The cruelest thing that can happen to you is for you to work to gain the world and then die and go to hell. That's the devil's wish for you.

Would you rather work your tail off climbing the corporate ladder into the cushy C-suite and die and perish, or live like a fool and die and perish? I hope the answer is neither, and that you would rather choose to live a life that matters by serving God. You will be able to leave a lasting impression by investing in God, His word, and His people.

Ecclesiastes 2:17 Therefore I hated life; because the work that is wrought under the sun is grievous unto me: for all is vanity and vexation of spirit.

Whenever a verse begins with the word "*therefore,*" it concludes the aforementioned points. In this case, the realization that the wise is no better than the fool in death has three affects on successful people whose hearts and affections are set on this world. (The phrase "*under the sun*" is repeated five times in verses 17–22 and a total of six times in *Ecclesiastes 2.*)

First, worldly focused successful people will hate life because all the work that is done under the sun is grievous and yields disappointment rather than expected happiness—"*for all is vanity and vexation of spirit.*" The word "*grievous*" in verse 17 is also translated as "evil" or "wicked," as in something that is so bad that we would label it "wicked".

Ecclesiastes 2:18 Yea, I hated all my labour which I had taken under the sun: because I should leave it unto the man that shall be after me. (19) And who knoweth whether he shall be a wise man or a fool? yet shall he have rule over all my labour wherein I have laboured, and wherein I have shewed myself wise under the sun. This is also vanity.

Second, worldly focused successful people will hate all their labor, because they are forced to surrender everything for which they have toiled over the years to their heirs.

After reaching the highest pitch of success, they soon realize their sun is setting and that they only have a small slice of time to enjoy the fruits of their labor before they must begin succession planning.

The word *"yea"* in verse 18 is affirmative and amplifies the notion of this hatred, in that they truly will hate all their labor. *Psalms 49:10 For he seeth that wise men die, likewise the fool and the brutish person perish, and leave their wealth to others. (11) Their inward thought is, that their houses shall continue for ever, and their dwelling places to all generations; they call their lands after their own names. (12) Nevertheless man being in honour abideth not: he is like the beasts that perish. (13) This their way is their folly: yet their posterity approve their sayings. Selah. (14) Like sheep they are laid in the grave; death shall feed on them; and the upright shall have dominion over them in the morning; and their beauty shall consume in the grave from their dwelling.*

Whatever proactive succession planning they might do in selecting the right people to manage their wealth, there is no guarantee that their heirs will be good stewards—*"who knoweth whether he shall be a wise man or a fool."* Yet their heirs will have full control over everything for which they have labored and wisely built over the years. This is vanity to the producer.

Some people think that it is easy to just give the wealth away. (These people have never built wealth with their own hands.) Since it takes so much time and effort to build wealth, the owners would want to hand their wealth over to people like themselves— people who not only are responsible, but also share their vision, philosophy, passion, tenacity, and discipline. Finding the right individuals is not easy. There is a good chance the inheritance will end up in the hands of fools.

There is a saying in my culture that wealth will not survive three generations. The first generation works very hard, saves, lives below their means, and does not spend on luxuries in order to raise an estate so that the second generation can have a better life. The third generation has a cushy life, never experiencing the hardship of the first generation, and never acquiring the wisdom to build wealth. They blow it away on luxuries, gambling, foolish investments, indulgences, etc. The things that the third generation does would cause the first generation to roll over in their graves. *Proverbs 27:24 For riches are not for ever: and doth the crown endure to every generation?*

Ecclesiastes 2:20 Therefore I went about to cause my heart to despair of all the labour which I took under the sun. (21) For there is a man whose labour is in wisdom, and in knowledge, and in equity; yet to a man that hath not laboured therein shall he leave it for his portion. This also is vanity and a great evil.

Lastly, worldly focused successful people will be disheartened and despair of all their labor under the sun, because it seems so unfair that they should have toiled so hopelessly—*"For there is a man whose labour is in wisdom, and in knowledge, and in equity; yet to a man that hath not laboured therein shall he leave it for his portion."* For them to labor so hard to acquire knowledge and skills and to ensure their works are equitable and right, and then to be forced to surrender everything to people who are clueless about their business, is vanity and a great evil, according to verse 21b.

If you are one of these worldly focused successful people, will you rejoice and pop champagne the day you are forced to turn over your estate? No, because after your death, the person celebrating the inheritance may be a fool who couldn't care less about your business.

Ecclesiastes 2:22 For what hath man of all his labour, and of the vexation of his heart, wherein he hath laboured under the sun? (23) For all his days are sorrows, and his travail grief; yea, his heart taketh not rest in the night. This is also vanity.

So what hope is there for worldly minded people who toil under the sun?

- *"All his days are sorrows"* – Life under the sun is sorrowful because of sin, and work is a distressing four-letter word. *Genesis 3:17 And unto Adam he said, Because thou hast hearkened unto the voice of thy wife, and hast eaten of the tree, of which I commanded thee, saying, Thou shalt not eat of it: cursed is the ground for thy sake; in sorrow shalt thou eat of it all the days of thy life.*

- *"His travail grief"* – Every business or task is not just grievous, but is grief itself.

- *"Yea, his heart taketh not rest in the night"* – Say hello to restlessness and sleepless nights. The word *"yea"* underscores this vexation. *Job 14:1 Man that is born of a woman is of few days, and full of trouble.*

Indeed, sorrow, grief, and restlessness are the reality of worldly minded people who seek happiness under the sun. The next time they think life sucks, what more can be said? By design, life under the sun is vain for those who serve self. (The word *"vanity"* [Hebrew הֶבֶל, pronounce as "heh'bel"] is used 30 times in the book of Ecclesiastes; eight times in *Ecclesiastes 2*.)

Ecclesiastes 2:24 There is nothing better for a man, than that he should eat and drink, and that he should make his soul enjoy good in his labour. This also I saw, that it was from the hand of God. (25) For who can eat, or who else can hasten hereunto, more than I? (26) For God giveth to a man that is good in his sight wisdom, and knowledge, and joy: but to the sinner he giveth travail, to gather and to heap up, that he may give to him that is good before God. This also is vanity and vexation of spirit.

With no prospect of true happiness from being wise or foolish, what is the best thing for earthly minded self-serving people to do with their life? Three things according to the above verses:

1. *"Eat and drink"*
   To those who refuse to serve God and choose this world for their lot, the goal in life is to eat and drink—the enjoyment of the present.

2. *"Make his soul enjoy good in his labour"*
   Self-servers under the sun should enjoy the profits and achievements of their labor (not someone else's labor), because every business effort is grievous and hard on the body. There is no point in hoarding riches, so use the gain from the labor and take comfort in it. At the end of a work day, throw a piece of meat on the grill and drink some beer. Repeat daily till death comes. *Ecclesiastes 3:22 Wherefore I perceive that there is nothing better, than that a man should rejoice in his own works; for that is his portion: for who shall bring him to see what shall be after him?*

3. See *"that it was from the hand of God"*
   God is kind. He extends His bountiful grace and provisions to people who refuse to serve Him; *"for he*

maketh his sun to rise on the evil and on the good, and sendeth rain on the just and on the unjust," according to *Matthew 5:45b.* These people should thank Him for strength, health, and the power to eat and enjoy the fruits of their labor. *Ecclesiastes 5:18 Behold that which I have seen: it is good and comely for one to eat and to drink, and to enjoy the good of all his labour that he taketh under the sun all the days of his life, which God giveth him: for it is his portion. (19) Every man also to whom God hath given riches and wealth, and hath given him power to eat thereof, and to take his portion, and to rejoice in his labour; this is the gift of God.* Even Solomon himself, with all his power and possessions, recognized that the capacity to enjoy earthly possessions was from God—*"For who can eat, or who else can hasten hereunto, more than I."*

Indeed, the only thing left for self-serving people to do in this world is enjoy the present. How sad it is for a precious life to be reduced to meaningless eating, drinking, and being merry—things that do not satisfy. That's what animals do; they live for today.

God can still get the glory from self-serving people who do not serve Him and who knock themselves out with worldly enjoyments. Verse 26 compares the blessings of those who are good in God's sight to the bad deal of sinners. (Verse 26 refers to self-serving people as sinners.) When rich sinners despair of ever finding happiness, they are moved to donate their wealth to those who are good before God. They may say something like, "We recognize the world has many challenges and we are in a unique position to make a significant positive impact. We feel a responsibility to share our good fortune, and we pledge the majority of our wealth over to this good cause." This also is vanity and vexation of spirit to the sinners, but God can use it to fund His causes. Read *Job 27:13-17, Proverbs 13:22.*

Final Thoughts

How do you feel about being on the same level as a fool who wastes his life on folly? How do you feel about turning over an estate that you diligently built over a lifetime to someone who does not share your vision and burden? These things are in store for you if you are busy pursuing earthly success and living for self with no accountability to the word of God.

Imagine, upon your demise, your company's public relations department releases this statement: "<Your name's> tremendous leadership, vision, and passion for the business had an impact on the community, the country, and the world. <Your name> not only transformed the industry, but also helped bring the city into the next century. We are tremendously proud of <your name's> legacy and will continue to work hard to live up to the unmatched standards <your name> set for excellence and integrity."

Could you stand before the Lord Jesus Christ, who died for your sins, with the above score card? How does it line up with God's mission? When you stand before God, He is not going to ask how well you did at your secular job. Your career is a means to an end, not an end in itself. That end ought to be ministry and fulfilling your duty to God in furthering His kingdom.

There is nothing wrong with having a successful career and living a comfortable and enjoyable life in this world. God is not against you becoming successful. If you read *Deuteronomy 8*, you will know that He wants to bless you abundantly. However, don't repeat the common mistake of pursuing a career and money before serving God. People who do this don't know when to stop. They make the first bundle of money and continue working for more because the nicer things of the world take hold of their hearts. The next thing they know, time and health slip away. It never works well when people put self before God. *Matthew 6:33 But seek ye first the kingdom of God, and his righteousness; and all these things shall be added unto you.*

Be not worldly rich and spiritually poor. Making a living and serving God are not mutually exclusive. If Jesus Christ is your Savior, the Bible says He bought you with a price. *1Corinthians 6:20 For ye are bought with a price: therefore glorify God in your body, and in your spirit, which are God's.* It is unwise to call on Jesus to be your sin bearer as if He is a mule without recognizing that He is your Lord, and that there will be a day of reckoning. By what standard are you going to account for your life at the Judgment Seat of Christ? That you raised a good family behind white picket fences?

Consider the words of the hymn, "Must I go, and empty-handed" by Charles C. Luther.

> Must I go, and empty-handed,
> Thus my dear Redeemer meet?
> Not one day of service give Him,
> Lay no trophy at His feet?
>
> Chorus:
> Must I go, and empty-handed?
> Must I meet my Savior so?
> Not one soul with which to greet Him:
> Must I empty-handed go?
>
> Not at death I shrink nor falter,
> For my Savior saves me now;
> But to meet Him empty-handed,
> Thought of that now clouds my brow.
>
> O the years in sinning wasted;
> Could I but recall them now,
> I would give them to my Savior,
> To His will I'd gladly bow.
>
> O ye saints, arouse, be earnest,
> Up and work while yet 'tis day;

Ere the night of death o'ertake thee,
Strive for souls while still you may.

Many successful Christians who love God see their workplace as a mission field. They are a beacon of light to their coworkers, helping them to see their need for a Savior. These brethren go to work each day to achieve a higher purpose. Others wake up each morning to go to work, work overtime, and work till they can work no more. Think about what you do daily; how much of those things matter in eternity? (The word of God and human souls last forever. Are you investing in them?)

No one will ever regret living for and serving Christ, but everyone will regret the years spent in vanity. How are you benefiting God's kingdom with your talents, success, and influence? Will you lead or champion a weekly Bible study in the workplace? Will you be a trusted spiritual counselor whom your coworkers can approach with questions or prayer requests? Let heaven celebrate your spiritual success. *Luke 15:10 Likewise, I say unto you, there is joy in the presence of the angels of God over one sinner that repenteth.*

Decide today that you will be salt and light at your workplace. Read *Matthew 5:13-16*. Do a good job, be trustworthy, nurture relationships, and pray for a door of utterance to share Christ with your coworkers. May God open your eyes and heart to their needs.

7 – Vanity of Human Industry

F orget serving God, how would you like to have your own utopia and live life on your terms? Make your life what you want it to be, do whatever you want, go wherever you want, and have everything your way. All you need is this one ability. Without it, you will be singing "Que sera, sera, whatever will be, will be."

Unless you have the ability to control destiny—have a plan and path to happiness that no one, not even God can ruin for you, your self-serving plan is in jeopardy.

Featured herein is a set of common life events and human activities to convince people that the buzzing human industry is not able to secure happiness against God's providence. The verses were made famous by the American rock band, "The Byrds" in their song "Turn, Turn, Turn."

Ecclesiastes 3:1 To every thing there is a season, and a time to every purpose under the heaven: (2) A time to be born, and a time to die; a time to plant, and a time to pluck up that which is planted; (3) A time to kill, and a time to heal; a time to break down, and a time to build up; (4) A time to weep, and a time to laugh; a time to mourn, and a time to dance; (5) A time to cast away stones, and a time to gather stones together; a time to embrace, and a time to refrain from embracing; (6) A time to get, and a time to lose; a time to keep, and a time to cast away; (7) A time to rend, and a time to sew; a time to keep silence, and a time to speak; (8) A time to love, and a time to hate; a time of war, and a time of peace. (9) What profit hath he that worketh in that wherein he laboureth?

"To every thing there is a season" is best understood as everything has a season (a window of time) of existence. For example, you exist for a season.

"A time to every purpose under the heaven" is best understood as when things happen or come into being for their intended purposes. Right off the bat, everything has a purpose. People like to quote, "Life exists for a purpose." Whose purpose? It is for God's purposes, not ours. The entire creation exists to bring honor and glory to the Lord Jesus Christ. *Revelation 4:11 Thou art worthy, O Lord, to receive glory and honour and power: for thou hast created all things, and for thy pleasure they are and were created.* People who live for self deny God the pleasure due Him and deny themselves of God's good purposes toward them. This recipe for happiness is madness.

God has a purpose for your life. Whatever that is, it is not in the form of you chasing after a good life, living comfortably behind white picket fences, raising good children, and calling it good. *Haggai 1:4 Is it time for you, O ye, to dwell in your cieled houses, and this house lie waste?* You are to put God first, take His yoke upon you, and endure hardness as a good soldier. *Matthew 11:29a Take my yoke upon you, and learn of me. 2Timothy 2:3 Thou therefore endure hardness, as a good soldier of Jesus Christ.* Wow, that's a far cry from the world's idea of happiness. (Relax, this is not to say you cannot enjoy life while doing the work of ministry. God is simply against you living a self-serving life.)

Notice that the word *"time"* occurs 29 times in verses 1 thru 8, for a total of 31 times in *Ecclesiastes 3*. Not only does everything happen for God's purposes, everything also happens in God's time. God determines when things come into being, how long they last, and the circumstances of their existence. But humans vehemently disagree. Nelson Mandela said, "I am the master of my fate and the captain of my destiny." Other quotes found on the internet include:

- "You are the master of your destiny. You can influence, direct, and control your own environment. You can make your life what you want it to be."

- "You are the architect of your own destiny; you are the master of your own fate; you are behind the steering wheel of your life. There are no limitations to what you can do, have, or be. Except the limitations you place on yourself by your own thinking."

Oh humans, seriously?!

We can't stand the fact that we are not the captain of our destiny, because that means our self-serving life is in jeopardy. We go all out to take control of our lives and master happiness through a hive of industry as listed in verses 2 thru 8 above.

However, verses 1 thru 8 set the stage for the thought-provoking question in verse 9 that challenges the capacity of human industry in delivering happiness— *"What profit hath he that worketh in that wherein he laboureth?"* How can one benefit toiling in an environment where people have no control over their destiny?

For consideration, Solomon presents 28 common human activities, which in reality are life events engineered by God. These life events, some good, some bad, some happy, and some sad, run their courses according to God's will, for He determines all human life affairs. We have no ability to pick out the benevolent and decline the brutal events. Calamities resulting from human violence and destruction—"a *time to kill,"* "a *time to weep,"* "a *time to mourn,"* "a *time of war,"* etc., which seem fortuitous and to be in the will of man are also determined by divine counsel. God in His sovereignty can distribute any event to anyone, and no one has the power to counteract. Take Job for example; God allowed evil to befall him, and there was nothing he could do about it. Read *Job 1, Job 2:1-10.* As such, we do not fear man, but God. And thank God for His merciful kindness, for the time to heal, laugh, dance, and peace that offset the bad times.

Since humans are unable to alter life circumstances against God's will, the question becomes, can self-serving people secure happiness without the ability to control their destiny? If not, then does it matter what work or activity these people do for happiness, whether they love or hate, build or demolish, and so on? The events in verses 2 thru 8 are extremes and polar opposites. It is God's way of challenging humans to go to the extremes and take their best shot at manufacturing happiness on their own.

The best case for self-serving people is to tip toe through life without adversities so that they can say, "I made it safely to the grave." Even so, it is a miserable and meaningless existence—a concoction that leads to hatred and depression. The things that they have to gain from a lifetime of labor are travail, misery, and sorrow with a bit of temporal enjoyment that does little good. Self-serving is simply not a good investment. Read *Ecclesiastes 2:11.*

Now, let's dive into the passage a bit more. Solomon begins with the season of life bracketed by *"a time to be born, and a time to die."* Humans can make babies, but God determines if and when the babies are born. *Genesis 21:1 And the LORD visited Sarah as he had said, and the LORD did unto Sarah as he had spoken. (2) For Sarah conceived, and bare Abraham a son in his old age, at the set time of which God had spoken to him.* Read *Genesis 17:21, Genesis 18:10-14.* Many couples plan careers before babies. While this is prudent, things may not go according to their plan, and they may not be able to conceive. It goes to show that they are not in charge of destiny and must submit to God's will.

God also determines every person's lifespan, because He is the giver and taker of all life. We don't have a say in when we will show up in this world and how long we get to live. Only God can extend a person's life, as He did for Hezekiah in *2Kings 20:1-11*.

"A time to plant, and a time to pluck up that which is planted"—Humans go about their agriculture activities, but God determines individual plant life: when a plant comes into existence, when it will be fruitful, and when it will be useless and uprooted. The agriculture example illustrates that humans must obey preordained seasons and times in order to properly enjoy God's providence. It emphasizes mankind's inability to affect the fixed condition of things and that in regard to happiness, one can only be happy by doing it God's way.

Both human and plant seasons of life have a beginning and ending, and a short lifespan with a proper growing period. In death however, harvested crops profit the grower, but self-serving people do not profit God, who gave them life, including every breath they take, every morsel they eat, and all their enjoyments. From God's perspective, vegetation is better, because He gets an output from the crop, but what output is there from the life of self-serving people? God receives more profit in crop farming than soul farming.

(Doctrinally, *"a time to pluck up that which is planted"* refers to people who do not have a personal relationship with Jesus Christ, as represented by the Pharisees in *Matthew 15:12*. God has a set time to uproot them. *Matthew 15:12 Then came his disciples, and said unto him, Knowest thou that the Pharisees were offended, after they heard this saying? (13) But he answered and said, Every plant, which my heavenly Father hath not planted, shall be rooted up.*)

"A time to kill"—Interestingly, the text goes from *"a time to plant"* to *"a time to kill,"* which reminds me of the story of Cain and Abel. *Genesis 4:2b Cain was a tiller of the ground. Genesis 4:8 And Cain talked with Abel his brother: and it came to pass, when they were in the field, that Cain rose up against Abel his brother, and slew him.* Subliminally, it communicates the wickedness of human

nature and the crookedness of their way in securing happiness. Read *Ecclesiastes 1:14-15*.

Yes, bad things happen to "good" people. (Biblically, there is none good, according to *Mark 10:18*. Truthfully, that only happened once, and the Son of God volunteered.) If God allows death to happen by way of murder or atrocity, what can one do? Since He brings us into the world, He can certainly take us out however He wants to. Because there is a time to every purpose under the heaven, God has a purpose for death. *Job 9:12 Behold, he taketh away, who can hinder him? who will say unto him, What doest thou? Job 11:10 If he cut off, and shut up, or gather together, then who can hinder him? 1Samuel 2:6 The LORD killeth, and maketh alive: he bringeth down to the grave, and bringeth up.*

"A time to heal"—If God in His mercy brings healing as He did to Job (*Job 42:12-17*), who can stop Him? *Malachi 4:2 But unto you that fear my name shall the Sun of righteousness arise with healing in his wings; and ye shall go forth, and grow up as calves of the stall. Hosea 6:1 Come, and let us return unto the LORD: for he hath torn, and he will heal us; he hath smitten, and he will bind us up. (2) After two days will he revive us: in the third day he will raise us up, and we shall live in his sight. Deuteronomy 32:39 See now that I, even I, am he, and there is no god with me: I kill, and I make alive; I wound, and I heal: neither is there any that can deliver out of my hand.*

"A time to break down"—If God allows a person or nation to break down, only He can reverse the course. We are watching America breaking down because of sins and the decay of its moral fabric. Unless we as a nation repent, everything we do to prop this country up is merely rearranging the deck chairs on the Titanic. *Job 12:14 Behold, he breaketh down, and it cannot be built again: he shutteth up a man, and there can be no opening.*

God has the power to prevent things from breaking down, according to the example in *Deuteronomy 29:5, "And I have led you forty years in the wilderness: your clothes are not waxen old upon you, and thy shoe is not waxen old upon thy foot."*

"A time to build up"—If God allows a person, corporation, or nation to be built up, that entity will prosper according to His will. The timing will be right and the resources will line up for the entity to seize the opportunity, even though some may attribute it to good fortune or luck.

"A time to weep"—If God orders the season of sorrow, even the strongest man will cry like a baby.

"A time to laugh"—When God gives the season of joy, laughter results. *Psalms 126:1 When the LORD turned again the captivity of Zion, we were like them that dream. (2) Then was our mouth filled with laughter, and our tongue with singing: then said they among the heathen, The LORD hath done great things for them. (3) The LORD hath done great things for us; whereof we are glad.*

As for the rest of the verses, you get the idea; it's "Que sera, sera, whatever will be, will be." Have you ever been in a streak of bad luck that you couldn't get out of no matter what you did? How many people can affect the outcome of life according to their terms? *Proverbs 16:9 A man's heart deviseth his way: but the LORD directeth his steps.* Human destiny is in God's hand, and there simply is no way for self-serving people to work out their own happiness. (For Christians, there is no such thing as luck, because God is in charge of everything. It is about His will.)

Ecclesiastes 3:10 I have seen the travail, which God hath given to the sons of men to be exercised in it.

Since everything exists for a purpose, the events in *Ecclesiastes 3:2-8* are extremes and polar opposites to the intent that they inflict maximum labor and misery to the workers. *Ecclesiastes 1:8a All things are full of labour; man cannot utter it.* Following Adam's sin, God sentenced mankind to hard labor that produces no happiness. *Genesis 3:19 In the sweat of thy face shalt thou eat bread, till thou return unto the ground; for out of it wast thou taken: for dust thou art, and unto dust shalt thou return.* The affliction of labor is a form of exercise. God is a great personal trainer who exercises mankind with travail so that humans may be weary of meaningless self-serving toil and choose to serve Him. Read *Matthew 11:28-30, Joshua 24:15.*

The travail of labor is synonymous with restless vexation and misery. One thing for sure, we will not ascribe happiness to the pains of labor.

Are you tired of planting and plucking, breaking down and building up, weeping and laughing, and casting away and gathering, yet? Is it time to serve God? *Matthew 11:28 Come unto me, all ye that labour and are heavy laden, and I will give you rest. (29) Take my yoke upon you, and learn of me; for I am meek and lowly in heart: and ye shall find rest unto your souls. (30) For my yoke is easy, and my burden is light.*

Ecclesiastes 3:11 He hath made every thing beautiful in his time: also he hath set the world in their heart, so that no man can find out the work that God maketh from the beginning to the end.

Everything that God does, including the seemingly awful travail that He assigns to mankind, will be beautiful in His time. But it is hard for humans to discern the beauty and harmony of God's works for three reasons:

1. They are stuck on the world—*"the world in their heart."*

We are naturally worldly minded and can only see the present, which is a mess.

2. They are stuck with limited knowledge—*"no man can find out the work that God maketh from the beginning to the end."*
   We are unable to acquire the knowledge of the full spectrum of God's work from the beginning to the end. *Ecclesiastes 8:17 Then I beheld all the work of God, that a man cannot find out the work that is done under the sun: because though a man labour to seek it out, yet he shall not find it; yea further; though a wise man think to know it, yet shall he not be able to find it.*

3. They are stuck with limited time—*"in his time."*
   Everything will be beautiful in God's time, not ours.

Even so, it hasn't stopped humans from trying to fix the contrary events that are in the world against God's providence. Without a complete knowledge and understanding of what God does from the beginning to the end, it is best for us to submit to Him and trust Him that everything will be beautiful in His time.

Everything that happens to unbelievers is to draw them to God. It is beautiful when one who is beaten up (exercised) by the world realizes that Jesus Christ is the better deal and by faith accepts Him as Lord and Savior for the pardoning of sins and gets to be with God in the perfect world to come.

Everything that happens to believers is to draw us closer to God. This includes life-threatening illnesses like cancer and tragedies like losing a loved one prematurely, but God has given us a beautiful promise that all things work together for good to them who love Him. No matter what we go through, it shall be well in the end. *Romans 8:28 And we know that all things work together for good to them that love God, to them who are the called according to his purpose. Deuteronomy 32:4 He is the Rock, his work is perfect: for all his ways are judgment: a God of truth and without iniquity, just and right is he.*

We typically do not see life-threatening cancer as God-sent and cannot comprehend the purpose of the affliction. Most of us are familiar with the Lazarus story, how that he died from a sickness and his sisters blamed Jesus for His tardiness. But Jesus said in *John 11:4b, "This sickness is not unto death, but for the glory of God, that the Son of God might be glorified thereby."* How wonderful and beautiful it was when Lazarus was resurrected to life. (All who die in Christ will be resurrected to life.)

Everything has a place and purpose in God's grand design. We need to understand that we are a piece of a beautiful picture puzzle. Every piece matters. It may be a dark, shadowy, and unglamorous puzzle piece, but it is necessary to complete the beautiful picture. I am not privy to the picture, but I am somewhat sure (I should be in the ballpark) that it tells the stories of creation, Lucifer's rebellion, the rise and fall of Adam, the redemption of mankind, the rise of the Jewish nation, the giving of the Law, the coming of the Messiah, His ministry, crucifixion, and resurrection, the church age, the rapture of the church, the Judgment Seat of Christ, the rise of antichrist, the Great Tribulation period, the second coming of Christ, the battle of Armageddon, the destruction of evil, the Great White Throne judgment, the lake of fire, the new heaven and earth, and Christ on the throne being worshipped by all creation. Now, which puzzle piece are you in this picture? In some cases, you get to decide because God has given you a free will. For example, you can decide not to be the piece in the lake of fire by accepting Jesus Christ as Lord and Savior for the forgiveness of your sins. You can also decide that by serving Him, you will not be the shameful piece at the Judgment Seat of Christ. (And if you also do not want your loved ones, relatives, or friends to be those pieces, then you should tell them about the good news of salvation in Jesus Christ and how to live for Him.) Other than that, you may chart your course, but what comes along the way and where you end up are up to God. *Proverbs 16:9 A man's heart deviseth his way: but the LORD directeth his steps.*

What is the smart thing to do in this case? Shouldn't it automatically trigger a healthy respect and fear of God, and compel you to serve and please Him out of reverence and love? You want to be on His good side, right?

Ecclesiastes 3:12 I know that there is no good in them, but for a man to rejoice, and to do good in his life. (13) And also that every man should eat and drink, and enjoy the good of all his labour, it is the gift of God. (14) I know that, whatsoever God doeth, it shall be for ever: nothing can be put to it, nor any thing taken from it: and God doeth it, that men should fear before him. (15) That which hath been is now; and that which is to be hath already been; and God requireth that which is past.

What happens when people fail to see the purposes of affliction and despair of the world? Those who do not get the point of the exercise will continue to serve self. They will set their affections on the things of the world and continue to hope in their labor, which is a one-way street to emptiness, hopelessness, and despair.

There are two things that people should know if they refuse to serve God:

1. Their labor will not secure them any lasting good—*"There is no good in them."* The best thing they can hope for from their labor is the enjoyment of the present—*"For a man to rejoice, and to do good in his life. And also that every man should eat and drink, and enjoy the good of all his labour, it is the gift of God."* How much they

can eat, drink, and enjoy is a gift from God. Humans are so not in control of their destiny.

2. Their labor will not alter the immutability of God's will concerning them. The sore travail that He has ordained for sinful mankind is not going away. And the same variety of life events will continue to befall every generation—*"That which hath been is now; and that which is to be hath already been; and God requireth that which is past."* It is futile to rely on human ingenuity to change the things that God has decreed. The proper response is to fear God and accept the travail as a gift, because it points people to Jesus Christ.

Final Thoughts

If you live for self, it makes sense that you base your happiness on your strength, wisdom, and ability to influence your destiny, and chalk unpleasant life events up to time and chance. But this philosophy is contrary to God's word and is torpedoed by the lessons in this chapter.

God orders our life events in order to accomplish His purposes and to show us that we are not in control of our destiny. As such, the self-serving life is unprofitable, because humans are unable to alter God's decrees no matter what they do. (You may provide God with good entertainment by telling Him the plan for your life.) *Isaiah 14:27 For the LORD of hosts hath purposed, and who shall disannul it? and his hand is stretched out, and who shall turn it back? Psalms 127:1 Except the LORD build the house, they labour in vain that build it: except the LORD keep the city, the watchman waketh but in vain. (2) It is vain for you to rise up early, to sit up late, to eat the bread of sorrows: for so he giveth his beloved sleep.*

Without the ability to control your destiny, who do you rely on for happiness? True or false: a dog's destiny is with its master, and a dog is happiest when it pleases its master.

As Christians, we say, "Jesus, you command my destiny." The devil cannot keep us from the will of God. We must come to the end of self and surrender the right to our lives to Him. We should live our lives in submission to His calling, sovereignty, providence, and will, having full assurance that His works are perfect, done in truth, honorable, glorious, powerful, merciful, righteous, and beautiful. (Submission is hard when there is a trust issue.) Read *Deuteronomy 32:4, Psalms 33:4, Psalms 111:3, Psalms 111:6, Psalms 145:9, Daniel 9:14, Ecclesiastes 3:11.* Jesus set a great example by submitting to the Father's will in the garden of Gethsemane. *Matthew 26:39 And he went a little further, and fell on his face, and prayed, saying, O my Father, if it be possible, let this cup pass from me: nevertheless not as I will, but as thou wilt.*

We exist for the purpose of serving and glorifying God in the seasons of our lives. If you are not yet serving Him, let this be a time of repentance. Will you own the Great Commission? Will you consider a mission field? Will you pray, prepare, give, or go as follows:

- Pray for God to give you a personal vision to be used for His kingdom. Ask Him to show you a field. (The field does not have to be overseas; it can be in your neighborhood, workplace, or a street corner.)

- Prepare for a short- or long-term mission by learning the word of God. You are responsible for understanding the gospel and must have a working knowledge of the Bible.

- Give to the cause of missions. Prayerfully set aside a certain amount above the tithe as an eternal investment.

- Visit a mission field and work alongside a missionary. You can write checks to missions, but there will come a time when you need to get your hands dirty. *Mark 16:15 And he said unto them, Go ye into all the world, and preach the gospel to every creature.* Read *John 4:35.*

Life for Christians is a decades-long boot camp in preparation for God's kingdom and government to come. Decide today to own the Great Commission and do the four points above so that you will have fruit to show at the Judgment Seat of Christ. May God bless you and make you fruitful.

8 – Vanity of Human Justice

There is a crisis happening across the world. A crisis so bad that the dead who are six feet under are happier than the living, and the happiest people are the unborn.

The world is awash in human injustice and oppression. No one can solve the problem as the fast-moving flood rages on unabated. Powerful, cruel, and heartless oppressors despair humanity with their exploitations, oppressions, and degradations, as God looks on passively. And the oppressed take it to the streets shouting, "We want justice, we want justice!"

Is there a relationship between justice and happiness? In Plato's masterpiece, "The Republic," book 10, section 612b, "...we have proved that justice in itself is the best thing for the soul itself, and that the soul ought to do justice..." If that's the case, then why do so many people all over the world still march for and demand justice? Why are some people met with the greatest wrongs in the courts to which they flee for justice? If Plato is right, can people whose lives are intrinsically tied to this world find happiness in a world of injustice?

Ecclesiastes 3:16 And moreover I saw under the sun the place of judgment, that wickedness was there; and the place of righteousness, that iniquity was there.

This verse begins with *"And moreover,"* which means this is yet another thing that impacts happiness that humans cannot overcome. In the previous chapter, Solomon sees the immutability of God's works and our inability to override God's will in an attempt to take charge of our destiny, and concludes that enjoying the present is the best course of action for self-serving people to do the rest of their lives. In this section, he sees wickedness in the court of law and sin in the court of morality, adding to the misery of mankind. In other words, not only are humans unable to overcome the acts of God, they also are unable to overcome the unjust acts of their fellows. Good luck with eradicating injustice from this world. Only God can do it. This is yet another example of humans' inability to take charge of their destiny.

No one should experience injustice firsthand. But there is no denying that the law is riddled with loopholes, and legal outcomes can be influenced and bought. Innocent people are sometimes wrongly convicted, while guilty people are acquitted. Often, politicians and judges are elected by special-interest groups with large campaign cash contributions. Whenever money is involved, judicial impartiality is a myth, and the laws are manipulated to create evasions for the guilty.

"The place of judgment" or courts have become a safe house for conspiracies and wickedness. *"The place of righteousness,"* where morality is expected, has become a safe house for immoral behaviors. (The sons of Eli were priests who abused the worshippers who went to the temple to sacrifice to God. *1Samuel 2:22 Now Eli was very old, and heard all that his sons did unto all Israel; and how they lay with the women that assembled at the door of the tabernacle of the congregation.*) Such is the nature of justice under the sun—the place self-serving people affectionately call home.

People who set their affections on this world must rely on its judicial system, which is broken and corrupt, for happiness.

Ecclesiastes 3:17 I said in mine heart, God shall judge the righteous and the wicked: for there is a time there for every purpose and for every work.

While God has a set time for judgment, when He will exonerate the just and condemn the wicked, it is yet in the future. In the mean time, you may be outraged by the oppression of innocent people and say to God, "Look at the afflictions and sufferings of the oppressed. Are you just going to sit and watch and do nothing? Why haven't you mopped up the injustices in this world?" Even the prophet Jeremiah complained to God about the prosperity of the wicked in *Jeremiah 12:1b, "Wherefore doth the way of the wicked prosper? wherefore are all they happy that deal very treacherously?"* Job likewise complained in *Job 21:7, "Wherefore do the wicked live, become old, yea, are mighty in power?"* Imagine the prayers of Christians in Muslim-majority countries. Imagine the prayers of the widows whose husbands were beheaded by the extremist militant group ISIS.

God delays His judgment for the following reasons:

1. We are not supposed to like this world.

2. To draw self-serving people to Him through the chastisement of tyranny and injustice. This is consistent with the way God dealt with the Jews who rejected Him in the Old Testament. *Psalms 106:41 And he gave them into the hand of the heathen; and they that hated them ruled over them. (42) Their enemies also oppressed them, and they were brought into subjection under their hand. Deuteronomy 31:17 Then my anger shall be kindled against them in that day, and I will forsake them, and I will hide my face from them, and they shall be devoured, and many evils and troubles shall befall them; so that they will say in that day, Are not these evils come upon us, because our God is not among us? (18) And I*

will surely hide my face in that day for all the evils which they shall have wrought, in that they are turned unto other gods. Read *Judges 2:14-15, Judges 3:8, 12-14, Nehemiah 9:26-27, 2Kings 21:10-15.*

3. People don't want God's justice anyway. They really want revenge according to what is right in their own eyes. Try telling these people that vengeance belongs to the Lord and that justice is love, mercy, and forgiveness. They will beat you and throw you out. So why should God be in any rush to clean up the injustices and oppressions in the world?

(Want real justice? Hint: *Psalms 89:14 Justice and judgment are the habitation of thy throne: mercy and truth shall go before thy face.*)

Let it be known that all power and authority in the world is appointed by God. No one can be in the position of power except God allows it. *Romans 13:1 Let every soul be subject unto the higher powers. For there is no power but of God: the powers that be are ordained of God.* God expects all who are in authority to do justly in their execution of judgment on the wicked. *Romans 13:3 For rulers are not a terror to good works, but to the evil.* This is a high bar for flawed human beings to achieve. Many are unfaithful in their discharge of duties, while others abuse the entrusted power and oppress the people they are appointed to serve and protect. Read *Matthew 20:25-28.*

Abusers of power beware; God cares about justice. *Proverbs 21:3 To do justice and judgment is more acceptable to the LORD than sacrifice.* God, the capital "J" Judge, shall review all judgments and shall judge both the righteous and the wicked, for He has appointed a time for righteous retribution. Read *Psalms 10:17-18, Psalms 73, Psalms 82:2, Isaiah 10:1-3.*

God's high expectations coupled with human weaknesses make power and authority a burden and a risk rather than an enjoyment. Being in power is a tremendous responsibility that often is not worth the worldly reward. The pay for many civil and religious servants is not commensurate with their responsibilities. Whether a person does it for pay or not, God's expectation is the same, and all who abuse their power will be judged and condemned. You should get your head checked if you aspire to power.

Ecclesiastes 3:18 I said in mine heart concerning the estate of the sons of men, that God might manifest them, and that they might see that they themselves are beasts. (19) For that which befalleth the sons of men befalleth beasts; even one thing befalleth them: as the one dieth, so dieth the other; yea, they have all one breath; so that a man hath no preeminence above a beast: for all is vanity. (20) All go unto one place; all are of the dust, and all turn to dust again. (21) Who knoweth the spirit of man that goeth upward, and the spirit of the beast that goeth downward to the earth?

Having seen the injustices in the world and humans' inability to properly handle power and authority, Solomon deflects his thoughts toward the estate of the *"sons of men"* (the condition of the people whose affections are set on the world, both the oppressed and the oppressors).

God allows such horrible oppressions in the world so that He may expose humans to themselves—that by choosing this world for their portion, they may see themselves on the same level as brute beasts. In living, they claw each other like beasts do, and both are powerless in controlling their destiny. In death, they have the same end state, with the exception of their spirit. *Psalms 49:12 Nevertheless man being in honour abideth not: he is like the beasts that perish. (20) Man that is in honour, and understandeth not, is like the beasts that perish.*

- Death happens to both of them – *"For that which befalleth the sons of men befalleth beasts."*

- They both have one breath or spirit, which is the energy of life – *"as the one dieth, so dieth the other; yea, they have all one breath."* When the spirit leaves the body, it is dead like a car without a battery.

- They both are vanity like vapor – *"so that a man hath no preeminence above a beast: for all is vanity."* When they die, it is as if they had never lived. These sons of men may think they are superior to beasts, but in this way, they are not.

- They both are of dust and return to dust – *"All go unto one place; all are of the dust, and all turn to dust again."*

In death, the trichotomy of the human nature becomes clear as the components separate. The body returns to dust, and the human spirit ascends and returns to God, who gave it. Animal spirits, however, go downward into the earth.

Where is the soul? It is missing from the text. This is because without a personal relationship with the Lord Jesus Christ, the souls of the sons of men will go downward like the spirits of beasts. Their souls will have no access to the source of spiritual light and life, and will be eternally separated from God. *John 8:12 Then spake Jesus again unto them, saying, I am the light of the world: he that followeth me shall not walk in darkness, but shall have the light of life.*

When people choose the world for their lot, it is easy to see that when all is said and done, they are no better than animals.

Ecclesiastes 3:22 Wherefore I perceive that there is nothing better, than that a man should rejoice in his own works; for that is his portion: for who shall bring him to see what shall be after him?

Given the above conditions, Solomon perceives that the best thing for worldly focused people to do is rejoice in their labor and enjoy the present (*Ecclesiastes 2:24, Ecclesiastes 3:12-13, Ecclesiastes 5:18-19, Ecclesiastes 8:15*), for this is their blessing, as tomorrow they may die and perish like a beast, after which they will not be able to return to see the aftermath. Read *Luke 16:19-31*, particularly verse 26. (Again, as mentioned in the previous chapter, how lamentable it is if your lot in life is reduced to rejoicing in your labor in the few years of your existence, because you love the world while the kingdom of God matters little to you. It is like saying, "Have fun at work." It's an oxymoron.)

Ecclesiastes 4:1 So I returned, and considered all the oppressions that are done under the sun: and behold the tears of such as were oppressed, and they had no comforter; and on the side of their oppressors there was power; but they had no comforter. (2) Wherefore I praised the dead which are already dead more than the living which are yet alive. (3) Yea, better is he than both they, which hath not yet been, who hath not seen the evil work that is done under the sun.

Following the digression, Solomon brings his thoughts back to the subject of the abuse of power. He considers all human oppression, including political, judicial, religious, and commercial, that takes place in the world from both sides—the oppressors and oppressed. He sees the absence of a comforter for both.

(Notice that injustice always leads to oppression. Injustice begins in *Ecclesiastes 3:16-17*, which is followed by oppression in *Ecclesiastes 4:1-3*.)

Oppressions take on various forms and are ubiquitous in the world today. Pope Francis, in his homily in St. Peter's Basilica, reflected on the "countless forms of injustice and violence which daily wound our human family." He said, "Sometimes we ask ourselves how it is possible that human injustice persists unabated, and that the arrogance of the powerful continues to demean the weak, relegating them to the most squalid outskirts of our world." He continued, "We ask how long human evil will continue to sow violence and hatred in our world, reaping innocent victims." (Source: "HOMILY OF HIS HOLINESS POPE FRANCIS", Vatican Basilica, Friday, January 1, 2016)

The oppressed innocent and helpless, who bewail their afflictions from cruel tribunals, and nefarious religious and business conducts that ruined their lives, and dissipated their wealth, have no one to pity, rally around, and comfort them. *Psalms 69:20 Reproach hath broken my heart; and I am full of heaviness: and I looked for some to take pity, but there was none; and for comforters, but I found none.*

The arrogant and heavy-handed oppressors also have no comforter to pacify them. Therefore injustice, oppression, and violence rage on. *Job 35:9 By reason of the multitude of oppressions they make the oppressed to cry: they cry out by reason of the arm of the mighty.*

The misery and cruelty of oppression is so bad that Solomon esteems the dead who are six feet under happier than the oppressed who are presently alive, because they have ended their miserable life. But happier than both is the unborn person who has not seen the evil work that is done under the sun. Of the three, who gets the short end of the stick?

If life is limited to this world only, it is better not to be born than to experience the vanity and evil under the sun only to perish in a Christless eternity. The worst case is being alive without a

Comforter and having to hope for worldly justice that is run by greedy and ungodly people.

Indeed, a Comforter—the Holy Spirit of God—is the solution for injustice and oppression. One gets the Comforter by accepting Jesus Christ as Lord and Savior. *John 14:16 And I will pray the Father, and he shall give you another Comforter, that he may abide with you for ever; (17) Even the Spirit of truth; whom the world cannot receive, because it seeth him not, neither knoweth him: but ye know him; for he dwelleth with you, and shall be in you. (18) I will not leave you comfortless: I will come to you.*

The unsaved world, by rejecting Jesus Christ, also rejects the Comforter. Consequently, they continue in their sufferings. Without the Comforter, there will be no real love, joy, peace, longsuffering, gentleness, goodness, faith, meekness, and temperance, because these things are the fruit of the Spirit. Read *Galatians 5:22-23.*

As Christians, we have the Comforter in us, who will comfort and strengthen us in the midst of fiery trials and tribulations. *2Corinthians 1:3 Blessed be God, even the Father of our Lord Jesus Christ, the Father of mercies, and the God of all comfort; (4) Who comforteth us in all our tribulation, that we may be able to comfort them which are in any trouble, by the comfort wherewith we ourselves are comforted of God.* Our Lord Jesus Christ also knows oppression all too well. He was oppressed by the wicked and therefore relates to our sufferings. *Isaiah 53:7 He was oppressed, and he was afflicted, yet he opened not his mouth: he is brought as a lamb to the slaughter, and as a sheep before her shearers is dumb, so he openeth not his mouth.*

Our hearts go out to unbelievers who suffer the terrible tragedy of injustice and oppression. Oh that they may reach out to Jesus Christ and be comforted. *Isaiah 19:20 And it shall be for a sign and for a witness unto the LORD of hosts in the land of Egypt: for they shall cry unto the LORD because of the oppressors, and he shall send them a saviour, and a great one, and he shall deliver them.*

Final Thoughts

Power and authority are ordained by God for the safety and comfort of communities, but without the fear of God and submission to the final authority (the word of God), wicked people will abuse power and pervert justice. *Proverbs 29:2 When the righteous are in authority, the people rejoice: but when the wicked beareth rule, the people mourn.*

The injustice and suffering in this world are so brutal that some would rather go straight from the womb to the grave. *Job 3:11 Why died I not from the womb? why did I not give up the ghost when I came out of the belly? Job 10:18 Wherefore then hast thou brought me forth out of the womb? Oh that I had given up the ghost, and no eye had seen me! (19) I should have been as though I had not been; I should have been carried from the womb to the grave.* If I could hold up a sign to the unborn, it would say, "Don't come here unless you will accept Jesus Christ as Lord and Savior."

If you do not know Jesus Christ as Lord and Savior, your only hope of justice is the world's corrupt and oppressive system, which you probably often complain about. Even Plato knew that happiness needs justice. But there is not enough justice in this world, so it is ludicrous to expect happiness from a vile world full of injustices.

If Jesus Christ is your Lord and Savior, you know that His name is the Prince of Peace. You have peace with God. *Romans 5:1 Therefore being justified by faith, we have peace with God through our Lord Jesus Christ.* You also have the Comforter, who is the Holy Spirit of God, to comfort you through trials and tribulations. Read *John 14:16-18.*

Fellow Christians, our goal is not to be happy and to tip toe through life so that we can say, "I made it to the grave without a scratch." We are to be useful to God and be concerned with His business. *John 14:12 Verily, verily, I say unto you, He that believeth on me, the works that I do shall he do also; and greater works than these shall he do; because I go unto my Father.* We are called to be joyful and to suffer for righteousness sake. Our joy is not in self, in a specific circumstance, or in the things of the world, because joy is a fruit of the Spirit, according to *Galatians 5:22*. When we make Christ the focus of life, we can be joyful even when we suffer persecution for our faith and uphold biblical values by speaking the truth.

It is helpful to be reminded of the following:

1. The price of righteous fellowship.
   We are called to partake in the fellowship of Christ's sufferings, according to *Philippians 3:10. 1Peter 2:21 For even hereunto were ye called: because Christ also suffered for us, leaving us an example, that ye should follow his steps.*

2. The price of righteous living.
   All who live godly will suffer persecution, because Satan is the god of this world, according to *2Corinthians 4:4.* Christians all over the world are persecuted for upholding biblical values and speaking the truth. Many lose their lives. *2Timothy 3:12 Yea, and all that will live godly in Christ Jesus shall suffer persecution. 1Peter 4:12 Beloved, think it not strange concerning the fiery trial which is to try you, as though some strange thing happened unto you.*

3. The price of righteous engagement.
   The reason God didn't take us to heaven the day we were saved is because we are to take up our cross and engage our spiritual enemy. As we rescue souls from the

devil's family through evangelism, it is reasonable to expect retaliation from the evil force. *1Thessalonians 3:3 That no man should be moved by these afflictions: for yourselves know that we are appointed thereunto. (4) For verily, when we were with you, we told you before that we should suffer tribulation; even as it came to pass, and ye know.*

Do you expect to be carried on a flowery bed of ease while others fight the battle and sail through bloody seas? Consider the words of the hymn "Am I a Soldier of the Cross?" by Isaac Watts.

Am I a soldier of the cross,
A follower of the Lamb?
And shall I fear to own His cause
Or blush to speak His name?

Must I be carried to the skies
On flowery beds of ease?
While others fought to win the prize,
And sailed through bloody seas?

Are there no foes for me to face?
Must I not stem the flood?
Is this vile world a friend to grace,
To help me on to God?

Sure I must fight, if I would reign
Increase my courage, Lord!
I'll bear the toil, endure the pain,
Supported by Thy word.

Thy saints, in all this glorious war,
Shall conquer, though they die;
They view the triumph from afar,
And seize it with their eye.

When that illustrious day shall rise,
And all Thy armies shine

In robes of victory through the skies,
The glory shall be Thine.

Will you have it any other way? Consider the Apostle Paul, who wrote the book of Philippians from his jail cell in Rome. He mentioned "joy" six times, "rejoice" 12 times, and "gladness" one time. Read about his sufferings in *2Corinthians 11:23-28* and his testimony in *Philippians 3:7-8. Romans 8:18 For I reckon that the sufferings of this present time are not worthy to be compared with the glory which shall be revealed in us.*

Can you say that your life matters and will count for the cause of Christ? Decide today that you will engage in God's mission as a good soldier of Christ and waste no more time living for self.

9 – Vanity of Human Enterprise

There seems to be a disorder that plagues the human occupations in this world. Skillful works yield envy instead of happiness. Hard work produces dissatisfaction. And the fruit of fame is doom.

God reveals in *Ecclesiastes 3* that we are not in charge of destiny and that the best thing for self-serving people to do in living out the rest of their days is to comfortably enjoy the present—eat, drink, and be merry. As usual, nobody cares for God's prescription, and people busy themselves manufacturing their own happiness.

Featured herein are three archetypes of self-serving people: an individual who hopes for happiness in skillful work; a solitary person who hopes for happiness by minding his own business, working hard, and hoarding riches; and a superstar king who hopes for happiness in fame. Will they succeed in securing happiness?

Ecclesiastes 4:4 Again, I considered all travail, and every right work, that for this a man is envied of his neighbour. This is also vanity and vexation of spirit. (5) The fool foldeth his hands together, and eateth his own flesh. (6) Better is an handful with quietness, than both the hands full with travail and vexation of spirit.

Would you rather have two handfuls with strife or one handful with quietness and tranquility of mind? Are you sure you are okay with just one handful? Do you not envy your friends who have much more? Look at the houses they live in, the cars they drive, and all their possessions. Don't you want to be like them?

Solomon considers all human toils for happiness, in particular the works of dexterity. His archetype is a dexterous person who works with his hands, meticulously doing everything right, and delivering quality work. His labor is wearisome, but he gains much—*"both the hands full."* He is successful, but his success draws envy. His hope of finding happiness through his skillful work vanishes, and he realizes it is empty and unsatisfying—*"vanity and vexation of spirit."* (If skilled work proves to be vanity and vexation of spirit, there is no hope in shoddy work to deliver happiness.)

Skillful and successful people will draw a certain amount of envy or jealousy from others. Unfortunately, the envy threshold has no definition and varies according to society. You will know it when you are bad-mouthed or when you hear insincere praise and sniping remarks, or are backstabbed by your "friends." Even so, that's benign, because envy can escalate into a full-blown deadly evil as it is rooted in evil, according to *James 3:13-16.* Envy can do more harm than wrath and anger. *Proverbs 27:4 Wrath is cruel, and anger is outrageous; but who is able to stand before envy?*

The other extreme is a lazy fool, who instead of working with his hands, folds them. He won't acquire the necessary skill to put food on the table. He is stricken and disquieted by hunger pangs and is so hungry that he could eat his arm.

Since the above extremes do not yield happiness, there is no point in emulating the gainful person whose labor is wearisome and is envied or the lazy fool who is plagued with hunger. *Ecclesiastes 4:6a* says, *"Better is a handful."* To get a handful, one must work and not fold the hands like the lazy fool. Again, it goes back to God's prescription for self-serving people to comfortably enjoy the fruit of their labor. It is better for them to lay hold on a handful with quietness and tranquility of mind than to work their tails off to gain many possessions that are spoiled by the envy of others.

The prescription is also good for Christians who serve God. *Proverbs 15:16 Better is little with the fear of the LORD than great treasure and trouble therewith. (17) Better is a dinner of herbs where love is, than a stalled ox and hatred therewith.*

What's your definition of a handful? What does that look like? Are you really convinced that *"better is an handful with quietness, than both the hands full with travail and vexation of spirit?"* If so, how does this affect your pursuit of worldly goods? A good prayer to pray is *Proverbs 30:7, "Two things have I required of thee; deny me them not before I die: (8) Remove far from me vanity and lies: give me neither poverty nor riches; feed me with food convenient for me: (9) Lest I be full, and deny thee, and say, Who is the LORD? or lest I be poor, and steal, and take the name of my God in vain."*

Ecclesiastes 4:7 Then I returned, and I saw vanity under the sun. (8) There is one alone, and there is not a second; yea, he hath neither child nor brother: yet is there no end of all his labour; neither is his eye satisfied with riches; neither saith he, For whom do I labour, and bereave my soul of good? This is also vanity, yea, it is a sore travail.

Solomon turns from considering the fruit of skillful work and sees another meaningless human effort, which is the pursuit of happiness in hoarding riches. His next archetype is a workaholic scrooge who disobeys God's prescription for the enjoyment of the present and expects to be happy by being rich and living in solitude. This scrooge is either a lone child or has severed ties with all family members and relatives so that no one will become a dependent and consume his wealth. It is all his. Even so, the scrooge can't stop working. He is focused on making more money and hoarding riches.

He is a slave to his business, working obsessively going from one opportunity to another. He is rich, but cannot find in his heart to live comfortably, because his eyes are not satisfied with his great wealth, driving him to labor endlessly for more riches. *Ecclesiastes 1:8 All things are full of labour; man cannot utter it: the eye is not satisfied with seeing, nor the ear filled with hearing.* He lives in pinching want amidst the greatest plenty. It doesn't cross his mind that he only has his own mouth to feed. This is vanity, a meaningless life that is also a sore travail, because he vexes himself to no purpose.

You probably are thinking, "That's not me, I am not a tightwad, and I know how to enjoy life." That's great, but are you living for self? Have you spent four to five hours this week (this month?) on kingdom work, or are you too busy pursuing the things of the world affecting no lives for Christ? The scrooge is the epitome of self-serving. He lives by the saying, "Get what you can, can what you get, and sit on the can." However, if this extreme model is miserable, there is no happiness in self-serving and hoarding riches, is there?

The problem with riches is the more of it people have, the more they want. Their eyes will not let them off the hook. They are always dissatisfied and work for more. Do you know of a very busy person who is happy? *Ecclesiastes 5:10 He that loveth silver shall not be satisfied with silver; nor he that loveth abundance with increase: this is also vanity.*

Tightwads don't think they are tightwads. They see themselves as responsible savers. Go ahead, work like a dog and hoard all the money in the world. In 100 years, who will be spending your money? Not you!

Ecclesiastes 4:9 Two are better than one; because they have a good reward for their labour. (10) For if they fall, the one will lift up his fellow: but woe to him that is alone when he falleth; for he hath not another to help him up. (11) Again, if two lie together, then they have heat: but how can one be warm alone? (12) And if one prevail against him, two shall withstand him; and a threefold cord is not quickly broken.

Partnership is better than going it alone. The scrooge who seeks happiness by increasing his wealth through solitary effort is defeated in his own game. The practical benefits of partnership, according to the above verses are as follows:

- Synergy – *"They have a good reward for their labour."* The synergy of two people produces a result that is greater than the sum of their individual efforts. Furthermore, two people can have a reciprocal relationship—a mutual or cooperative interchange of favors and privileges.

- Mutual aid – *"For if they fall, the one will lift up his fellow."* Remember the TV commercial line, "I've fallen, and I can't get up!"? There is no need to buy the advertised gadget if there is a partner to solve the problem. It is extremely important to have partners in ministry in case one falters. Jesus sent His disciples out two by two, according to *Mark 6:7.* Who is your ministry partner who prays and labors with you?

- Comfort – *"If two lie together, then they have heat."* Imagine two people cuddling up in winter months.

- Protection – *"If one prevail against him, two shall withstand him."* The united strength of two people (a two-fold cord) is a better defense against an enemy. But a three-fold cord provides a much better defense. Smart people will have the Lord as the third cord in their relationship.

Ecclesiastes 4:13 Better is a poor and a wise child than an old and foolish king, who will no more be admonished. (14) For out of prison he cometh to reign; whereas also he that is born in his kingdom becometh poor. (15) I considered all the living which walk under the sun, with the second child that shall stand up in his stead. (16) There is no end of all the people, even of all that have been before them: they also that come after shall not rejoice in him. Surely this also is vanity and vexation of spirit.

Caution! We are entering an obscure and ambiguous zone in scripture. The above verses have been taken in very different ways. Nonetheless, they communicate a clear message—the vanity of fame, even for a king. The people's affections for the reigning prince are temporary, because it is human nature to gravitate to new things, in this case, a new legitimate successor or an upstart challenger. This is known as the worship of the rising sun.

How rare it is to find a wise child. It is like finding a large and perfect blue diamond. "Wise" and "child" typically don't go together, because foolishness is bound in the heart of a child and wisdom usually comes with age. *Job 32:7 I said, Days should speak, and multitude of years should teach wisdom.* What's more, this child comes from a poor background that cannot afford a good education and tutors. And to make this archetype even more extreme, this child comes out of prison to reign. In other words, this child comes from a zero-privilege environment compared to the king who has all privileges. Such a wise child is very rare. It is much easier for an old king to become a fool than for a child to be wise. Naturally, this extraordinary success gives hope to many—*"There is no end of all the people, even of all that have been before them."* His success story is covered in the news and in magazines all over the world, and he gets the "Person of the Year" award.

The bad news is, like everything else in this world, his popularity also is temporal—*"they also that come after shall not rejoice in him."* He will be eclipsed by new and uprising stars as people divert their affections to worship the rising sun. A reign that begins so famously ends in obscurity. *Proverbs 27:24 For riches are not for ever: and doth the crown endure to every generation?*

If this kind of extreme rare success and fame does not deliver happiness, the garden variety kind does not stand a chance. Fame is vain. The fruit of fame is doom. Never rely on fame for happiness.

Note:
Some scholars interpret the *"second child"* in verse 15 as a third character, in addition to the poor and wise child and the old and foolish king. This view is problematic, because it leaves the story of the poor and wise child dangling with no closure or conclusion.

Final Thoughts

The fruit of skillful work is envy; the fruit of hard work and hoarding is dissatisfaction; and the fruit of fame is doom. Do you stand a chance of finding happiness in a secular occupation?

This is not to say you should ditch your job for full-time ministry. Not everyone is called to be an ordained minister, but everyone is a minister of the word of God.

- Jesus entrusted us with the gospel. *1Thessalonians 2:4 But as we were allowed of God to be put in trust with the gospel, even so we speak; not as pleasing men, but God, which trieth our hearts.*

- Jesus gave us the ministry of reconciliation and sends us as ambassadors to the world. *2Corinthians 5:17 Therefore if any man be in Christ, he is a new creature: old things are passed away; behold, all things are become new. (18) And all things are of God, who hath reconciled us to himself by Jesus Christ, and hath given to us the ministry of reconciliation; (19) To wit, that God was in Christ, reconciling the world unto himself, not imputing their trespasses unto them; and hath committed unto us the word of reconciliation. (20) Now then we are ambassadors for Christ, as though God did beseech you by us: we pray you in Christ's stead, be ye reconciled to God.*

- Jesus ordained us to be fruitful. *John 15:16 Ye have not chosen me, but I have chosen you, and ordained you, that ye should go and bring forth fruit, and that your fruit should remain: that whatsoever ye shall ask of the Father in my name, he may give it you.*

God is in the business of reconciling the world to Himself by Jesus Christ. Take pleasure in co-laboring with Jesus in the Father's business of soul farming—sowing the seeds of righteousness (the word of God) and reaping souls for His kingdom. Adam failed to multiply and replenish the earth with righteous souls, so Jesus came to reboot the job. *Luke 19:10 For the Son of man is come to seek and to save that which was lost.* We play a part in this through evangelism (from personal evangelism to church planting). Jesus says in *Luke 5:32, "I came not to call the righteous, but sinners to repentance."* Evangelism is not reserved for gifted evangelists. It is what all Christians are called to do. Evangelism must be the passion of our hearts and the pursuit of our prayers.

Jesus also discipled common people. *Matthew 4:19 And he saith unto them, Follow me, and I will make you fishers of men.* He started with 12 disciples, and they taught others who were faithful. This is discipleship. *2Timothy 2:2 And the things that thou hast heard of me among many witnesses, the same commit thou to faithful men, who shall be able to teach others also.* In this case, it goes from Paul to Timothy, to faithful men, to others—a total of four generations.

Are you able to articulate the salvation gospel and lead sinners to Christ? Are you able to disciple young believers? If not, these should be your immediate goals. May God equip you for His service and prosper you with fruit that remains.

The one work that will pay off in the future is the work of the Lord. *1Corinthians 15:58 Therefore, my beloved brethren, be ye stedfast, unmoveable, always abounding in the work of the Lord, forasmuch as ye know that your labour is not in vain in the Lord.*

10 – Vanities in Divine Service

I s there happiness in religious rites? What's in it for people who faithfully perform religious duties? Is there an act that yields more happiness than others?

There are four vanities in divine worship that are related to the hand-foot-and-mouth disease and have nothing to do with the Coxsackievirus A16. Millions of people have contracted this disease and are worshipping God in vain, their success destroyed. People should absolutely avoid these four vanities in divine worship.

Ecclesiastes 5:1 Keep thy foot when thou goest to the house of God, and be more ready to hear, than to give the sacrifice of fools: for they consider not that they do evil.

What do fools do to look good? They need a form of godliness, so they go to the house of God, albeit to perform **vain religious exercises**, because they have the spiritual hand-foot-and-mouth disease. They are not mindful of their walk (foot disease). They don't consider their evil deeds or sinful lifestyle and are unrepentant of their sins. For example, how many unmarried church attendees sleep with their significant others?

Fools are quick to give **vain offerings** (hand disease). They love to give charitable donations, hoping to gain brownie points with God by their outward performance and hypocritical devotion like the Pharisees in *Matthew 6:1-4.* They don't know what God says concerning giving, because their ears are not attentive to hearing His words. So they give God things that are not important to Him—

"the sacrifice of fools." Proverbs 15:8 The sacrifice of the wicked is an abomination to the LORD: but the prayer of the upright is his delight.

Keep the following three things in mind when worshiping God:

- Be mindful of your walk.
  Twice God says in the book of *Haggai*, *"Consider your ways."* (*Haggai 1:5, 7*) If you are not right with God, repent and ask for forgiveness. You will find that He is gracious, longsuffering, and ready to forgive. *Proverbs 28:13 He that covereth his sins shall not prosper: but whoso confesseth and forsaketh them shall have mercy.* One thing you do not want to do is mock God with your disobedience. *Galatians 6:7 Be not deceived; God is not mocked: for whatsoever a man soweth, that shall he also reap. 1Samuel 15:22 And Samuel said, Hath the LORD as great delight in burnt offerings and sacrifices, as in obeying the voice of the LORD? Behold, to obey is better than sacrifice, and to hearken than the fat of rams.*

- Be ready to hear what God has to say.
  This reminds me of the story in *Nehemiah 8:1-12* when the Jews were attentive to hearing the words of the law read by Ezra the priest. They were convicted by the words they heard and were sorry for their sins. Thereafter, they were comforted. The hearing of the word was a necessary part of the cleansing process. *James 1:19 Wherefore, my beloved brethren, let every man be swift to hear, slow to speak, slow to wrath.* Read *Proverbs 4:20-27.*

- Bring the right sacrifice.
  o *Psalms 51:16 For thou desirest not sacrifice; else would I give it: thou delightest not in burnt offering.*

(17) The sacrifices of God are a broken spirit: a broken and a contrite heart, O God, thou wilt not despise.

o   *Romans 12:1 I beseech you therefore, brethren, by the mercies of God, that ye present your bodies a living sacrifice, holy, acceptable unto God, which is your reasonable service. (2) And be not conformed to this world: but be ye transformed by the renewing of your mind, that ye may prove what is that good, and acceptable, and perfect, will of God.*

Ecclesiastes 5:2 Be not rash with thy mouth, and let not thine heart be hasty to utter any thing before God: for God is in heaven, and thou upon earth: therefore let thy words be few. (3) For a dream cometh through the multitude of business; and a fool's voice is known by multitude of words.

Fools pray **vain prayers** (mouth disease). They do not search their hearts before speaking to God, but are impulsive with their mouths in uttering wordy and vain prayers. *Matthew 15:8 This people draweth nigh unto me with their mouth, and honoureth me with their lips; but their heart is far from me.* They do not consider what comes out of their big mouths or the consequences, because their hearts are hasty to utter things before God. While they speak out of the abundance of their hearts, they do not realize that nothing good can come out of their evil and deceitful hearts. *Matthew 12:34 O generation of vipers, how can ye, being evil, speak good things? for out of the abundance of the heart the mouth speaketh. (35) A good man out of the good treasure of the heart bringeth forth good things: and an evil man out of the evil treasure bringeth forth evil things. (36) But I say unto you, That every idle word that men shall speak, they shall give account thereof in the day of judgment. (37) For by thy words thou shalt be justified, and by thy words thou shalt be condemned.*

Because the mouth is connected with the heart, fools also have heart disease on top of hand-foot-and-mouth disease. This combination will no doubt get them into a lot of trouble with God.

Fools also are inconsiderate of their position relative to God's. God is holy and righteous, while they are vile creatures. God is in heaven and they are on earth, which is His footstool. None in their right mind would be rash with the mouth and ramble before an earthly king, what more before the King of kings. Fools are like little yappy dogs on the ground barking up a storm, which always draws a "shut up!" reaction from people—*"let thy words be few."*

Have you ever heard people praying in repetitions? It's supposed to be a prayer, not a chant. *Matthew 6:7 But when ye pray, use not vain repetitions, as the heathen do: for they think that they shall be heard for their much speaking.* And then there are those with rapid-fire, incoherent gibberish words to God. They think they have acquired a heavenly language. They spray instead of pray. Good communication is not in the quantity of words, but quality. Babbling is not communication.

Fools' prayers are wordy and as vain as a dream. Busy activities in the daytime yield dreams at night, which are nothing. Likewise, fools' wordy prayers amount to nothing.

While prayers are open channels of communication to God, and we can boldly approach His throne (*Hebrews 4:16*) to talk with Him as between friends, we should not be hasty in saying anything to Him. We live in a culture that conditions us to be hasty in our communication. We want to be the first to post things on social media. Our prayers need to be the product of the meditation of our hearts that is filtered through our thoughtful minds before leaving our mouths. Prayers may be lengthy, but need not be wordy, rambling, or long-winded, because God knows our needs before we even ask, according to *Matthew 6:8*.

Ecclesiastes 5:4 When thou vowest a vow unto God, defer not to pay it; for he hath no pleasure in fools: pay that which thou hast vowed.

Fools pledge **vain vows**. They love to vow or make pledges to God, especially when they are in a jam. They are quick to give lip service, "God, if you will do this for me, I will..." But when God does His part, they conveniently forget about their vows and go on with their lives, or make excuses in delaying. God does not take lightly to such mockery from fools—*"he hath no pleasure in fools."*

Imagine you ask your buddy for help to load some heavy stuff into your truck and promise to treat him to pizza. But after loading, you say to your buddy, "I am kinda busy now. I will catch you later." How do you think your buddy feels?

A vow is a bond upon the soul. *Numbers 30:2 If a man vow a vow unto the LORD, or swear an oath to bind his soul with a bond; he shall not break his word, he shall do according to all that proceedeth out of his mouth.* Vows are voluntary self-imposed sacrifices. There is no requirement to vow, but once made, it becomes a bond. Anyone who vows to God needs to speedily and cheerfully pay in full. (The word "pay" occurs three times in verses 4 and 5, to underscore the seriousness of fulfilling one's vow.)

Ecclesiastes 5:5 Better is it that thou shouldest not vow, than that thou shouldest vow and not pay.

Due to the serious nature of a vow and the weak human flesh, it is better for a person not to vow to God than to vow and not pay up. Don't misunderstand this verse. It does not say one should never vow. The issue is to vow and not pay.

Be very careful when making promises stemming from a sudden emotional passion. Do not make deals with God. Do not offer to do something in return for something. Guard your heart and mouth; it is not good to have a rash mouth and a hasty heart. *Proverbs 21:23 Whoso keepeth his mouth and his tongue keepeth his soul from troubles. Proverbs 12:13 The wicked is snared by the transgression of his lips: but the just shall come out of trouble.* The reason God gives us two ears and one mouth is so that we will be more ready to hear His words than to speak. An Ethiopian proverb says, "The fool speaks, the wise man listens."

Ecclesiastes 5:6 Suffer not thy mouth to cause thy flesh to sin; neither say thou before the angel, that it was an error: wherefore should God be angry at thy voice, and destroy the work of thine hands? (7) For in the multitude of dreams and many words there are also divers vanities: but fear thou God.

At issue here is the mouth disease—a rash mouth that is quick to make thoughtless promises to God. Hasty vows can lead to sin and all kinds of vanities. This includes vows with low chances of getting fulfilled through the frailty of the flesh, such as vows of celibacy without the gift of being single, or for an alcoholic to vow never to drink again. Read about Jephthah's sad story in *Judges 11:30-40*. His vow caused him to sacrifice his own daughter.

The person who vows has no excuse to not perform it. Any attempt to nullify a vow as if it was made in error is adding sin upon sin. One cannot say, "I didn't mean it," or "I wasn't thinking right when I made that vow." Therefore, it is highly advisable to not shoot one's mouth off before God and risk His anger and judgment. It goes back to verse 5, "*Better is it that thou shouldest not vow, than that thou shouldest vow and not pay.*"

(Note: "*The angel*" in verse 6 refers to the Lord Jesus Christ, who sometimes is called "*the angel of the LORD,*" or "*the angel of God.*")

As dreams are vanities, so are excuses that are made for the non-performance of vows. Excuses do not invalidate vows. All these problems could be avoided if people feared God more and talked less. For example, a woman is unhappy because she married a loser and makes all kinds of excuses to get out of the marriage. Well, if she had followed God's prescription for what type of person she should date and marry, she would not be in this predicament. But now she is stuck with her vow and the loser for the rest of her life.

Ecclesiastes 5:8 If thou seest the oppression of the poor, and violent perverting of judgment and justice in a province, marvel not at the matter: for he that is higher than the highest regardeth; and there be higher than they. (9) Moreover the profit of the earth is for all: the king himself is served by the field.

In conclusion, people should just keep their mouths shut and fear God, because He punishes sin. *Proverbs 17:28 Even a fool, when he holdeth his peace, is counted wise: and he that shutteth his lips is esteemed a man of understanding.* Unfortunately, most people can't shut up. When they see oppressions and gross injustices (the robbing or plundering of the poor), they will run off at the mouth wondering how God could allow such awful things to happen to good people and not avenge them. They don't understand that God has checks and balances in place as follows:

- *"For he that is higher than the highest regardeth; and there be higher than they."*
  According to verse 8, the plundering of the poor is committed by authority at the province level. God has put in place a hierarchy of authorities. There are authorities who will watch over the highest superior of each province, and there are higher authorities yet, all the way leading up to God Himself.

- *"Moreover the profit of the earth is for all: the king himself is served by the field."*

  It has been much debated whether this verse should be connected with verse 8 or 10. Since it begins with *"moreover,"* it makes sense to me that it is connected to verse 8. Even so, it is difficult to explain this verse. The idea is that everyone, including the king, is sustained by the field, so there is a limit to the oppression of the poor who own and work the fields. Ultimately God cares for the poor. *Proverbs 22:22 Rob not the poor, because he is poor: neither oppress the afflicted in the gate: (23) For the LORD will plead their cause, and spoil the soul of those that spoiled them. Proverbs 22:16 He that oppresseth the poor to increase his riches, and he that giveth to the rich, shall surely come to want.*

Final Thoughts

Rightness with God is not about getting a religion or performing religious rites. It comes from a right relationship with His Son, Jesus Christ. *John 14:6 Jesus saith unto him, I am the way, the truth, and the life: no man cometh unto the Father, but by me.*

A New York billionaire businessman is so confident in the eternal value of his contributions to charities that he said that when he gets to heaven's Pearly Gates, he will be so well known by his good works that God will straightway let him in without an interview. This successful businessman is tragically misinformed regarding the means to a proper relationship with God. He will not make it to heaven. Pray for him to see and accept the truth.

If you live life with no knowledge of or accountability to God's word, but desire a form of godliness, there is a good chance you will just be going through the religious motions and worshiping

God in vain. Beware of the spiritual hand-foot-mouth-and-heart disease.

Did you promise God anything? Do you have an outstanding or delinquent vow or pledge to pay? Now is the time to fulfill it. How about that marriage vow that you made before God? Are you living up to it?

How about things that you didn't promise but should be doing? That's part of being a family. There are chores that you don't have to promise to do, you just have to do them. Evangelism and discipleship are two such things. If God takes no pleasure in fools, do you think He takes pleasure in His disobedient children? Self-serving children of God are like teenagers who live under their parents' roofs, but don't listen, obey, or help.

Decide today that you will learn to present the gospel of salvation. Learn the "Romans Road" approach for leading people to the Lord and memorize the verses. When you get this down, you will be able to lead people to the Lord, and that is fruit to your account at the Judgment Seat of Christ. May God give you the heart of an evangelist and bless you with fruit that remains.

11 – Vanity of Wealth

Hello people who are obsessed with being rich. Five traps await you. Two of the traps are wicked. Read this before charging at the pot of riches.

Featured herein is an extreme case of covetousness for worldly riches to show that if such an extreme effort to collect wealth does not yield happiness, there is no hope for less enthusiastic wealth-seekers.

This chapter covers *Ecclesiastes 5:10* thru *Ecclesiastes 6:12* and can be outlined as follows:

- The vanity of wealth in securing happiness – *Ecclesiastes 5:10-17.*
- The vanity of wealth without use – *Ecclesiastes 5:18 – 6:12.*

Ecclesiastes 5:10 He that loveth silver shall not be satisfied with silver; nor he that loveth abundance with increase: this is also vanity.

Leading the way is the trap of **dissatisfaction** for people who love money. (The word *"silver"* is also translated as "money," as it is a form of money.) They are defeated by the very thing that they hope to secure happiness in.

Money is a medium of exchange in the form of coins and banknotes. What kind of person will you be if money buys happiness? Will you be a spender or saver? Neither. You will be a hoarder of money, because it is about spending power. Your happiness is tied to the amount of money you have. Furthermore, your happiness is in worldly elements because money can only procure worldly things.

Money in and of itself is not the problem, but the love of money is the root of all evil, according to *1Timothy 6:10*. There is nothing wrong with having a lot of money, if you have the wisdom to manage it. You will get into trouble when you don't have enough money and become infatuated with what it could do for you. You will replace God with a sad substitute called "cash".

Most people would not admit they love money. *1Timothy 6:8-10* gives the profile of a money lover:

- A person who is not content with food and raiment – *1Timothy 6:8*.
- A person whose goal is to be rich – *1Timothy 6:9*.
- A person who covets money – *1Timothy 6:10*.

Money, when pursued as an obsession or chief good, is as addictive and as anticlimactic as drugs and alcohol that destroy lives. Like drug addicts who hope to be satisfied with the next high, people who love money think they will be happy if they can have more of it. In some cultures, such as the one yours truly is from, the answer to most of life's problems is more money. In Southeast Asia, one can pretty much say, "The answer is more money. What's the question?" Covetousness is a way of life. The truth is that money lovers will never be satisfied with money.

Happiness does not lie in money or in the abundance of possessions. If you have accumulated some money, you know money does not satisfy you. It's a one-way love affair. Happiness lies in a right relationship with the Lord Jesus Christ. This is a simple truth, but how does one get this wisdom into the heads and hearts of people who are supercharged on the world? They will not receive this wisdom and will repeat the same foolish mistakes as their predecessors. This is unfortunate, because the realization of this vanity usually happens late after people have spent most of their productive years chasing after worldly riches that are dissatisfying. Enrollment in the school of hard knocks is automatic when people refuse to do what's right for them according to God's prescriptions. *1Timothy 6:9 But they that will be rich fall into temptation and a snare, and into many foolish and hurtful lusts, which drown men in destruction and perdition.*

We live in a money-crazed world. The Bible instructs us to flee from the desire to be rich and the love of money to a life with a higher goal. *1Timothy 6:11 But thou, O man of God, flee these things; and follow after righteousness, godliness, faith, love, patience, meekness. (12) Fight the good fight of faith, lay hold on eternal life, whereunto thou art also called, and hast professed a good profession before many witnesses.* The Bible also cautions us not to serve money. *Matthew 6:24 No man can serve two masters: for either he will hate the one, and love the other; or else he will hold to the one, and despise the other. Ye cannot serve God and mammon.* How much money would it take for you to betray your relationship with the Lord Jesus Christ? Judas Iscariot did it for 30 pieces of silver.

Will you trade your heavenly rewards for worldly riches? While salvation is not earned, heavenly rewards are based on performance and are earned through your service to the Lord. By not serving the Lord, you will lose heavenly rewards. Worldly losses are temporal, but heavenly losses are permanent. The fruit of your labor for the kingdom of God can be gold, silver, and precious stones (representing the deity of Christ or the word of God, the price of redemption, and human souls), or wood, hay, and stubble, which are worldly things that burn away at the Judgment Seat of Christ. *1Corinthians 3:11 For other foundation can no man lay than that is laid, which is Jesus Christ. (12) Now if any man build upon this foundation gold, silver, precious stones, wood, hay, stubble; (13) Every man's work shall be made manifest: for the day shall declare it, because it shall be revealed by fire; and the fire shall try every man's work of what sort it is. (14) If any man's work abide which he hath built thereupon, he shall receive a reward. (15) If any man's work shall be burned, he shall suffer loss: but he himself shall be saved; yet so as by fire.*

Don't get ripped off by the world. May God open your eyes to see the real treasure in Christ. Read *Psalms 19:7-11, Proverbs 3:13-18, Proverbs 8:10-11, Revelation 3:17-18.*

Ecclesiastes 5:11 When goods increase, they are increased that eat them: and what good is there to the owners thereof, saving the beholding of them with their eyes?

Like magic, worldly riches are a **disappearing** act, because riches come with baggage known as additional support and maintenance. *Proverbs 23:5 Wilt thou set thine eyes upon that which is not? for riches certainly make themselves wings; they fly away as an eagle toward heaven.*

Here is the dilemma of people who hope for happiness in the abundance of riches. (As mentioned above, these people automatically become hoarders of money and will not consume their wealth.)

- It is foolish for them to not enjoy life, because it is short.

- While it is good for them to upgrade their lifestyle, this comes with additional expenditures, because an entourage of dependents—children, relatives, friends, and strangers—will come out of the woodwork to feed on the wealth. And some of the dependents eat like a horse.

Covetous individuals will have the pleasure of feasting their eyes on their goods and bank account balances, but will have the displeasure of watching others feasting on their wealth. They gnash their teeth in dissatisfaction.

Do you know of a covetous person who doesn't complain about life? Take this principle to heart: *"When goods increase, they are increased that eat them."* Consider Jesus' counsel in *Luke 12:15*, *"And he said unto them, Take heed, and beware of covetousness: for a man's life consisteth not in the abundance of the things which he possesseth."*

Ecclesiastes 5:12 The sleep of a labouring man is sweet, whether he eat little or much: but the abundance of the rich will not suffer him to sleep.

Sleep is the ultimate rest, according to *Psalms 127:2*, but riches have an insomnia effect. The *"laboring man"* who doesn't earn much as a blue-collar person has a better night's sleep than the rich covetous person with abundance of goods. The laboring man's sleep is so much better, because he is physically worn out and has less to lose.

While rich people can afford many things, quality slumber may not be on the menu because of the cares and worries. Money can buy a comfortable bed, but not sleep. Do you know of rich and famous people who have to take drugs to sleep? Some have died from overdoses.

Worldly riches can be burdensome and **disquieting,** especially for those whose hearts are inordinately set on money. They stress and worry about protecting and growing their assets. Not having good quality sleep can lead to health issues. What good are riches then?

The key to having restful nights when riches increase is in *Psalms 62:10b, "If riches increase, set not your heart upon them."* This is quite an impossible feat for those whose worth is defined by their riches.

Ecclesiastes 5:13 There is a sore evil which I have seen under the sun, namely, riches kept for the owners thereof to their hurt. (14) But those riches perish by evil travail: and he begetteth a son, and there is nothing in his hand.

The practice of hoarding riches is so bad that it is classified as *"sore evil"* or wicked. The issue here is *"riches kept,"* instead of being enjoyed. See verse 18 below.

In some Asian cultures, the current generation is extremely driven to ensure the prosperity of the next generation. The parents hoard riches with a great deal of care so that their descendants can have a better life.

The dissatisfaction of riches drives them to want more and compels them in the way of fast, risky, and illegal money. Their appetite for risk and reward increases. They don't care about what's right or moral. They just want a lot of money fast. *Proverbs 28:22 He that hasteth to be rich hath an evil eye, and considereth not that poverty shall come upon him.* Their dissatisfaction leads to poor judgment and evil business, which ultimately costs them everything. Their estates **disintegrate**.

What seems to be a promising money-making endeavor in building an estate that can be passed on to the next generation can suddenly collapse due to the greedy misconduct of the hoarders. The unjust methods of obtaining riches cost the hoarders everything, and they are left with nothing to pass on to their heirs. *Proverbs 13:11 Wealth gotten by vanity shall be diminished: but he that gathereth by labour shall increase. Proverbs 11:24 There is that scattereth, and yet increaseth; and there is that withholdeth more than is meet, but it tendeth to poverty.* The practice of hoarding ends up hurting instead of helping the next generation. In a way, the sins of the parents are visited upon the children.

Covetousness is a sin of idolatry that invites the judgment of God. *Colossians 3:5 Mortify therefore your members which are upon the earth; fornication, uncleanness, inordinate affection, evil concupiscence, and covetousness, which is idolatry: (6) For which things' sake the wrath of God cometh on the children of disobedience.*

Ecclesiastes 5:15 As he came forth of his mother's womb, naked shall he return to go as he came, and shall take nothing of his labour, which he may carry away in his hand. (16) And this also is a sore evil, that in all points as he came, so shall he go: and what profit hath he that hath laboured for the wind? (17) All his days also he eateth in darkness, and he hath much sorrow and wrath with his sickness.

A financial disaster is an unbearable blow to many money hoarders. Some would choose to end their lives. The favorite method of committing suicide in Asia is to jump off an apartment high rise. When I was in college in Kuala Lumpur, there was a 17-story apartment building that was frequently used for this purpose.

Even if financial disaster does not take its toll on money hoarders, death eventually will. Worldly riches have a term limit. Death strips people of their wealth, and there is nothing these covetous people can take with them. Immediately after their last breath, their riches depart from them and their net worth crashes to zero. *Psalms 49:17 For when he dieth he shall carry nothing away: his glory shall not descend after him.*

What makes this **displacing** trap such a *"sore evil"* or wicked is that people can spend their entire life hoarding riches that do not satisfy and end up losing their soul. These people have a full schedule every day of the week and take no time to consider the forgiveness of sin and the gift of life from Jesus Christ. They come into this world naked and a sinner and depart likewise—*"in all points as he came, so shall he go." Mark 8:36 For what shall it profit a man, if he shall gain the whole world, and lose his own soul?*

Consider Jesus' remark regarding those who trust in uncertain riches. *Mark 10:24 And the disciples were astonished at his words. But Jesus answereth again, and saith unto them, Children, how hard is it for them that trust in riches to enter into the kingdom of God! (25) It is easier for a camel to go through the eye of a needle, than for a rich man to enter into the kingdom of God.*

Oh that covetous people would realize that they are laboring for the wind. There is much labor, but in the end, there is no profit. These people live and die miserably. They are so focused on raising an estate that they kill themselves with labor—*"All his days also he eateth in darkness."* The next thing they know, they are laying flat in a hospital bed, and get this, they are upset with the timeout because they can't be out there making more money—*"he hath much sorrow and wrath with his sickness."*

You may be thinking, "That's not me, I am not that extreme." True, most people are not this extreme, but if your focus is "me and my," you are related to the covetous person featured herein. Both have a me-centric mindset. Your schedule does not have room for kingdom work, and your life testifies that the treasures of the world are better than the treasures of heaven. Furthermore, if such extreme measures of hoarding riches is vanity, your estate has no chance of yielding happiness.

Below is a quick recap of what's in it for extreme hoarders of riches:

- Unable to find satisfaction in riches – verse 10.
- Unable to find in their hearts to consume their wealth – verse 11.
- Unable to get a good night's sleep – verse 12.
- Unable to pass on the wealth – verse 13-14.
- Unable to take their wealth with them in death – verse 15.

Ecclesiastes 5:18 Behold that which I have seen: it is good and comely for one to eat and to drink, and to enjoy the good of all his labour that he taketh under the sun all the days of his life, which God giveth him: for it is his portion. (19) Every man also to whom God hath given riches and wealth, and hath given him power to eat thereof, and to take his portion, and to rejoice in his labour; this is the gift of God. (20) For he shall not much remember the days of his life; because God answereth him in the joy of his heart.

Compared to the anxious life of covetous hoarders, self-serving people should enjoy God's providence before they die. They should go ahead and use what they have according to their allotment in life. God has given them a portion, which is a life measured in days (to emphasize the brevity of it) to labor under the sun. They should expect to labor, and for their own good, should eat, drink, and enjoy the fruits of their labor for their comfortable passage through this world.

God blesses certain self-serving hoarders with riches and wealth and gives them the *"power to eat"* (capacity to enjoy the good life). He enables them to take up their portions and rejoice in what they do. These people have an easier passage through life and will not much remember the toilsome and sorrowful days, because God gives them gladness. However, let not these people think that they are special, because God is sovereign, and He does what He pleases. Read *Psalms 135:6, Psalms 115:3, Isaiah 46:10, Daniel 4:35.* Let them acknowledge that God is good.

Ecclesiastes 6:1 There is an evil which I have seen under the sun, and it is common among men: (2) A man to whom God hath given riches, wealth, and honour, so that he wanteth nothing for his soul of all that he desireth, yet God giveth him not power to eat thereof, but a stranger eateth it: this is vanity, and it is an evil disease.

To drive home the message of vanity of riches without use, Solomon points to an evil that is common or falls heavily upon hoarders. Compared to the people in *Ecclesiastes 5:18-20*, whom God blesses and gives the power to eat, the people in this passage are also blessed to the point their *"cup runneth over,"* but God takes away the power to eat and gives it to strangers instead. *Proverbs 16:33 The lot is cast into the lap; but the whole disposing thereof is of the LORD.* These people hoard riches and would not use their wealth. In the end, their wealth is disposed to strangers and not their heirs. (Again, this shows that humans are not in charge of destiny. God decides every individual's lot in life. No one has the ability to overrule the order of providence.)

The practice of hoarding riches is a common evil disease that must be repented of. It arises from a corrupt heart. Hoarding was also common in Solomon's days when there was no reason to hoard riches when peace, quietness, and silver and gold abounded. Read *1Chronicles 22:9, 1Kings 10:27.*

The "Panama Papers" documents, leaked in 2015, reveal that more than 360,000 people and companies hide their hoards of illegal wealth in offshore accounts. A "USA Today" article headline reads, "Welcome to the biggest global corruption scandal in history." The article says, "It's a data dump bigger than Wikileaks. An enormous trove of 11.5 million documents from a law firm in

Panama, 'Mossack Fonseca,' shows an unprecedented pattern of global corruption that goes back 40 years." (This is just data from one firm. There are many other companies out there that service hoarders.)

Ecclesiastes 6:3 If a man beget an hundred children, and live many years, so that the days of his years be many, and his soul be not filled with good, and also that he have no burial; I say, that an untimely birth is better than he. (4) For he cometh in with vanity, and departeth in darkness, and his name shall be covered with darkness. (5) Moreover he hath not seen the sun, nor known any thing: this hath more rest than the other. (6) Yea, though he live a thousand years twice told, yet hath he seen no good: do not all go to one place?

If extreme hoarders are further blessed with a large family and a long life, but are too stingy to enjoy their wealth, to the point that they don't even provide themselves a decent burial plot, then a stillborn is preferred over them.

In Eastern cultures, the wealthy pick their burial grounds according to Feng Shui or geomancy. They shell out a lot of money for good burial plots. The burial plot of the founder of Resorts World Genting in Malaysia comprises an entire mountain. He purchased and established it before his death. Google "Memorial Hall Genting Highlands" for more information. A wealthy person who dies without preselecting and prepurchasing a burial plot is the talk of the town. People shake their heads in disbelief.

Hello hoarders, if life is limited to this world only, the fate of a miscarried fetus, who is carried from the womb to the grave, is better than yours. How do you feel that a nameless stillborn, who never sees the light of day or experiences the world, has more rest than you—*"do not all go to one place?"*

You may live 1,000 years—make that 2,000 years—but you are miserable every day and don't enjoy the good of your labor. Since you are not joyful in the day of prosperity, you are also not joyful in the day of adversity. And because you have no hope beyond this life, your end game is to die and perish. What difference will it have made how long you lived, who you were, and how much you were worth?

Ecclesiastes 6:7 All the labour of man is for his mouth, and yet the appetite is not filled. (8) For what hath the wise more than the fool? what hath the poor, that knoweth to walk before the living?

Here are more reasons why it is vanity and folly to hoard riches and expect happiness from it.

There are people who labor for worldly riches that only gratify the physical body. What difference does it make if a rich person eats caviar and a poor person eats chicken feet? Both are content when the stomach is full, and both will be hungry again. Both souls remain dissatisfied. (The word "*appetite*" is also translated as "soul.") Where is the advantage of riches?

No amount of riches can satisfy the deepest longing of the soul. At the physical level, the wise person has no advantage over the fool, because the fool gets the same pleasure in stuffing his face regardless of what he eats. And the rich is no better than the poor who knows how to properly conduct his life, because he too will have food, clothing, and shelter.

It doesn't take much to meet the body's physical needs. What's the point in hoarding riches? A good prayer to pray to God is, *Proverbs 30:7 Two things have I required of thee; deny me them not before I die: (8) Remove far from me vanity and lies: give me neither poverty nor riches; feed me with food convenient for me: (9)*

Lest I be full, and deny thee, and say, Who is the LORD? or lest I be poor, and steal, and take the name of my God in vain.

Ecclesiastes 6:9 Better is the sight of the eyes than the wandering of the desire: this is also vanity and vexation of spirit.

We would be happier to be content with and enjoy what we presently have than to let our desire wander and covet things we don't have. The world says, "Gain is godliness." It pushes us to focus on and long for inconsequential things that do not satisfy, and hence is vanity. The wandering of desire creates discontentment and vexes the spirit.

God says, "Godliness with contentment is great gain." Read *1Timothy 6:5-6.*

Ecclesiastes 6:10 That which hath been is named already, and it is known that it is man: neither may he contend with him that is mightier than he. (11) Seeing there be many things that increase vanity, what is man the better? (12) For who knoweth what is good for man in this life, all the days of his vain life which he spendeth as a shadow? for who can tell a man what shall be after him under the sun?

All efforts for riches cannot impart lasting happiness, because we are the sons of Adam with known traits—fallen, sinful, vile, and wretched. The richest people in the world, with all the things that their wealth can afford, are just humans and not God. *Psalms 9:20 Put them in fear, O LORD: that the nations may know themselves to be but men. Selah.* Read *Romans 9:20, Job 9:1-4.*

Humans, in their best state, are vanity and worth less than nothing. *Psalms 39:5 Behold, thou hast made my days as an handbreadth; and mine age is as nothing before thee: verily every man at his best state is altogether vanity. Selah. Isaiah 40:17 All nations before him are as nothing; and they are counted to him less than nothing, and vanity.*

Furthermore, mere mortal humans who are no more than a few handfuls of dust, have no ability to contend with God to improve the vanity of worldly riches to their favor.

Worldly riches are just one of the many things that increase vanity. People who set their affections on the world will desire and accumulate things that ought to be able to make them happy, but in reality, those things work in reverse. They only increase vanity and misery. What advantages do these people have in this environment? What worldly things can they further accumulate to make them happy? None. They will be no closer to true happiness with an abundance of things.

This world is a minefield for people who are ignorant of God's word. They do not know what's good for them or how to live a meaningful and fulfilled life. As such, they waste the precious little time they have busying themselves in things of no eternal reward, and in the end, their lives amount to nothing—*"all the days of his vain life which he spendeth as a shadow." Proverbs 14:12 There is a way which seemeth right unto a man, but the end thereof are the ways of death.* They are also ignorant of their future state. They trust in their wealth and boast themselves in the multitude of their riches, as if their legacy will continue forever. That's a false hope. The truth is that they will never know what will become of their riches after their death—*"for who can tell a man what shall be after him under the sun?"*

Final Thoughts

If your affections and hopes of happiness are set on the world, money will naturally become your idol, because it gives you all that your heart desires. This leads to the love of money and hoarding—a trap that drowns people in destruction and perdition, which is your undoing.

Are you wealthier than Solomon? If you are counting on the next million dollars for happiness, you are running an experiment that has been proven to disappoint. Money is a terrible god and is a corrupt substitute for true happiness. Anyone who serves money is serving the wrong master.

If your wealth is all you are worth, you are worth nothing after your last breath. (I'm being generous. According to *Isaiah 40:17*, you are worth less than nothing.) In the afterlife, there is only one accountant who determines your net worth, and He is God. Do you know His accounting method? What are you worth when you stand naked before Him—stripped of your good looks, strength, knowledge, wealth, all worldly possessions, and self righteousness? It doesn't pay to live as if there is no hereafter with no riches toward God. By serving Christ, you establish your eternal worth with God.

This does not mean Christians cannot be worldly rich. (In some circles, there is a tendency to demonize rich people. It is good to have rich brothers and sisters in Christ. They can take on projects that people who are in debt cannot.) Praise God if you are wealthy. You can create a purpose for your wealth and support righteous causes.

Again, money is not the root of evil, but the love of money is. The goal in life is not to be rich, but to be a good and faithful custodian of God's resources. Read *Matthew 25:14-30* to find out which servant you are in the story. Beware of the deceitfulness of riches, which can choke the blessed word of God that is sown in your heart and make you unfruitful. *Matthew 13:22 He also that received seed among the thorns is he that heareth the word; and the care of this world, and the deceitfulness of riches, choke the word, and he becometh unfruitful.*

Since you cannot take earthly treasures with you in death, would you like to convert them to heavenly treasures in your account so that you will have them when you get there? Did you know you can start making deposits in heaven? *Matthew 6:19 Lay not up for yourselves treasures upon earth, where moth and rust doth corrupt, and where thieves break through and steal: (20) But lay up for yourselves treasures in heaven, where neither moth nor rust doth corrupt, and where thieves do not break through nor steal: (21) For where your treasure is, there will your heart be also.* Will you join me in funding mercy and truth projects for the furtherance of the kingdom of God? (Truth without mercy is cruel. Mercy without truth is social work.) Meet the physical needs of the people (mercy) for the purpose of sharing the gospel of Jesus Christ (truth) with them. You can start this project yourself or partner with a church or missionary. Drought usually grips India between March and May. You can supply drinking water and partner with local pastors to preach the gospel. Famine and malnutrition plague parts of Africa. You can supply food and partner with local pastors to show the love of Christ and preach the gospel. Humanitarian needs abound; make sure it is mercy and truth, and not just a social work. Also make sure to budget your finances to accommodate this kind of kingdom work. As Christians, we must take care to fund and advance missions and not spend like unsaved people who live for the present and have no hope beyond this life. A good prayer is *Psalms 119:36, "Incline my heart unto thy testimonies, and not to covetousness."*

The eternal fruits from your labor and investments ought to make you very satisfied and happy. *Ephesians 2:10 For we are his workmanship, created in Christ Jesus unto good works, which God hath before ordained that we should walk in them.* May God richly bless you with true riches.

12 – Remedy for Vanities

A priceless W-word is the best antidote for the vanities in this world. All the things that may be desired are not to be compared to it. *"It cannot be gotten for gold, neither shall silver be weighed for the price thereof. It cannot be valued with the gold of Ophir, with the precious onyx, or the sapphire. The gold and the crystal cannot equal it: and the exchange of it shall not be for jewels of fine gold. No mention shall be made of coral, or of pearls: for the price of <u>wisdom</u> is above rubies. The topaz of Ethiopia shall not equal it, neither shall it be valued with pure gold. (Job 28:15-19)"*

When God essentially gave Solomon a blank check in Gibeon (*1Kings 3:5-13*), Solomon wrote "wisdom" on it. Therefore it's not surprising that Solomon offers wisdom as the answer to his question in *Ecclesiastes 6:12, "For who knoweth what is good for man in this life, all the days of his vain life which he spendeth as a shadow?"* In *Ecclesiastes 7*, he gives the instructions of wisdom for specific situations, as outlined below:

- Wisdom for overcoming the vanity of life under the sun – *Ecclesiastes 7:1-6.*
- Wisdom for dealing with oppressions and injustices – *Ecclesiastes 7:7-10.*
- Wisdom for enjoying an inheritance – *Ecclesiastes 7:11-12.*
- Wisdom for handling evil days – *Ecclesiastes 7:13-14.*
- Wisdom for living out a life grant – *Ecclesiastes 7:15-18.*
- Wisdom for coping with emotional injury – *Ecclesiastes 7:19-22.*

- Wisdom for avoiding sinful temptations – *Ecclesiastes 7:23-29*.

Ecclesiastes 7:1a A good name is better than precious ointment;

The key to overcoming the vanity of life under the sun is to live life with death and the Judgment Seat of Christ in mind. This includes:

1. Procuring a good name – *Ecclesiastes 7:1a*.
2. Making frequent deposits into your heavenly bank account – *Ecclesiastes 7:1b*.
3. Releasing the heart that is fixed on the world – *Ecclesiastes 7:2-4*.
4. Hearing the rebuke of the wise – *Ecclesiastes 7:5-6*.

Will your legacy be a good name or great riches? (*"Precious ointment"* is very costly and represents worldly riches. Read *John 12:3*.) Which do you think will endure? The scent of a precious ointment may linger for awhile, but will eventually fade away.

God says in *Proverbs 22:1*, *"A good name is rather to be chosen than great riches, and loving favour rather than silver and gold."* He also says in *Proverbs 27:24*, *"For riches are not for ever: and doth the crown endure to every generation?"* But the world says, "Gain is godliness," which means profits and riches trump a good name or reputation. Get riches, by hook or by crook.

Does it make sense to live this temporal life focusing on amassing wealth, only to die and perish? In the afterlife, *"The memory of the just is blessed: but the name of the wicked shall rot,"* according to *Proverbs 10:7*. No amount of precious ointment can mask the stench.

What is a good and enduring name for the afterlife? Will the names Michael, Gabriel, or Mary make the cut? No, only one name will endure forever. The name Jesus Christ is above all names and will endure forever. *Philippians 2:9 Wherefore God also hath highly exalted him, and given him a name which is above every name: (10) That at the name of Jesus every knee should bow, of things in heaven, and things in earth, and things under the earth; (11) And that every tongue should confess that Jesus Christ is Lord, to the glory of God the Father. Psalms 135:13 Thy name, O LORD, endureth for ever; and thy memorial, O LORD, throughout all generations.* Read *Psalms 49:10-14, Matthew 6:9b.*

If you do not know Jesus Christ as Lord and Savior, you are in Adam. His name stands for disobedience and death. As a descendant of Adam, you do not have hope beyond this life. *1Corinthians 15:22 For as in Adam all die, even so in Christ shall all be made alive.*

If by faith you trust Jesus Christ as Lord and Savior, you are in Christ. As such, your name is written is the book of life. All your sins are forgiven, and you will spend eternity with God in heaven.

One thing is for sure, you do not want to die in Adam. You also do not want to die in Christ and appear spiritually barren at the Judgment Seat.

The #1 way to overcome the vanity of life is to secure a good and righteous name—Jesus Christ—and serve Him and bear spiritual fruit. *Acts 4:12 Neither is there salvation in any other: for there is none other name under heaven given among men, whereby we must be saved.*

Ecclesiastes 7:1b The day of death than the day of one's birth.

If the day of death is better than the day of one's birth, then we should pray, "O God, please kill me today," right? Of course not. But how does this verse make sense and to whom does it apply?

Most people celebrate birthdays instead of the day of death. But Solomon says, *"The day of death"* is better than *"the day of one's birth."* The statement is paradoxical and goes against conventional wisdom. In *Ecclesiastes 4:2*, he esteems the dead who are six feet under happier than the people who are alive, because they have ended their misery.

For unsaved people, whose lives are limited to this world only, this makes sense, because the day of death is the end of their misery on earth. (Emphasize "on earth," because a new reality and misery await them after they draw their last breath. They leave the frying pan for the fire.) So they hang on to their miserable lives as long as they can. For them, to live is miserable and to die is horrible.

For Christians, to live is Christ—to do the will of the Father. For those who have fought a good spiritual fight, finished the course, and kept the faith, as the Apostle Paul, the day of death is better than the day of their birth, because to die is gain. *Philippians 1:21 For to me to live is Christ, and to die is gain. (22) But if I live in the flesh, this is the fruit of my labour: yet what I shall choose I wot not. (23) For I am in a strait betwixt two, having a desire to depart, and to be with Christ; which is far better: (24) Nevertheless to abide in the flesh is more needful for you.* Read *2Timothy 4:6-8*.

My day of birth was bad, because I came into this world a sinner, but I am going out as a son of God. It is well with my soul. In the meantime, I should be doing the following before meeting my Maker.

The #2 way to overcome the vanity of life is to send ahead to the Judgment Seat of Christ—make frequent deposits into your bank account in heaven by sharing the gospel and winning souls for the kingdom of God and discipling young believers. This is the gold, silver, and precious stones, which represent the deity of Christ, the word of God, and the souls of men that *1Corinthians 3:12* wants us to bring to the Judgment Seat of Christ. Without them, we will have nothing to show and will appear before God as naked as a jaybird and smelling like a bonfire, because *1Corinthians 3:13* says, *"Every man's work shall be made manifest: for the day shall declare it, because it shall be revealed by fire; and the fire shall try every man's work of what sort it is."* We are judged according to our usefulness to God. The Judgment Seat of Christ will be a terrifying, shameful, and regretful time for people who abuse the grace of God and appear before the King of Kings and Lord of Lords empty handed. They will realize His great sacrifice and their great selfishness. Read *1Corinthians 3:11-15, 2Corinthians 5:10-11.*

We were drafted into God's army when we received Christ as Savior. Do you think our engagement is optional? *2Timothy 2:3 Thou therefore endure hardness, as a good soldier of Jesus Christ. (4) No man that warreth entangleth himself with the affairs of this life; that he may please him who hath chosen him to be a soldier.*

Let your day of death be better than your day of birth and the celebration of your departure be a great gain to God's kingdom.

Ecclesiastes 7:2 It is better to go to the house of mourning, than to go to the house of feasting: for that is the end of all men; and the living will lay it to his heart.

The #3 way to overcome the vanity of life is to release the heart that is fixed on the world as follows:

1. Visit the dead – *Ecclesiastes 7:2.*
2. Embrace sorrow – *Ecclesiastes 7:3.*
3. Leave your heart in the house of mourning – *Ecclesiastes 7:4.*

If you receive conflicting invitations: one to a fun party with good food and drinks, and the other to a funeral service, you should attend the latter, because your heart will be better. The word "heart" appears four times in verses 2 thru 4.

The funeral service will put you in the right state of mind to lay to heart the end of life—that the wages of sin is still death, and no one can take anything away from a lifetime of labor under the sun. The sight of the corpse in an open casket, the tears of loved ones and friends, the solemn conversations, the somber and pensive mood of the service, and the final goodbye will cement the reality of life in this world. It causes reflection on human frailty and mortality, the fleetingness and vanity of life, and the importance of a right standing with God. Suddenly a life lived for Christ vs. self is more serious. *Deuteronomy 32:28 For they are a nation void of counsel, neither is there any understanding in them. (29) O that they were wise, that they understood this, that they would consider their latter end!*

No funeral to go to? How about visiting a graveyard?

Ecclesiastes 7:3 Sorrow is better than laughter: for by the sadness of the countenance the heart is made better.

Embrace sorrow. While laughter is good medicine, sorrow is God's prescription for hearts that are set on the world.

A heartfelt sorrow brought about by the contemplative experience in the house of mourning is good, because God is dealing with the heart, drawing it to Him. *Psalms 119:67 Before I was afflicted I went astray: but now have I kept thy word. Psalms 119:71 It is good for me that I have been afflicted; that I might learn thy statutes.*

Ecclesiastes 7:4 The heart of the wise is in the house of mourning; but the heart of fools is in the house of mirth.

Life has ups and downs. One of the differences between the wise and the fool is in the placement of the heart. Wise people place their hearts in the house of mourning. Even though they may not physically be there, their minds constantly reflect upon the end state of life and the hereafter. It humbles them and helps them set a right focus and priority in life. *James 4:9 Be afflicted, and mourn, and weep: let your laughter be turned to mourning, and your joy to heaviness. (10) Humble yourselves in the sight of the Lord, and he shall lift you up.*

The heart of fools is in the house of mirth. Their minds are occupied with the levity and pleasures of the senses. But as we learned in *Ecclesiastes 2:1-2*, this is vanity. As such, fools are ill equipped to deal with the downs of life, and they crash and burn. They also do not consider their eternal welfare, living life as if there is no God and no hereafter. *Psalms 14:1 The fool hath said in his heart, There is no God. They are corrupt, they have done abominable works, there is none that doeth good.*

Ecclesiastes 7:5 It is better to hear the rebuke of the wise, than for a man to hear the song of fools. (6) For as the crackling of thorns under a pot, so is the laughter of the fool: this also is vanity.

The #4 way to overcome the vanity of life is to hear the rebuke of the wise. Are your ears open to godly reproofs that may hurt your feelings, or are they more open to songs of fools that don't edify?

The jovial laughter of fools is as the crackling of ignited thorns under a pot. The dried thorns catch fire quickly, flash-burn fiercely, make much noise, and end suddenly. Its short-lived nature makes it inappropriate fuel for making a meal, which is the intended activity in verse 6. Hence, the happiness of excited fools is vain, as it is not long-lasting. *Job 20:4 Knowest thou not this of old, since man was placed upon earth, (5) That the triumphing of the wicked is short, and the joy of the hypocrite but for a moment? (6) Though his excellency mount up to the heavens, and his head reach unto the clouds; (7) Yet he shall perish for ever like his own dung: they which have seen him shall say, Where is he? (8) He shall fly away as a dream, and shall not be found: yea, he shall be chased away as a vision of the night. (9) The eye also which saw him shall see him no more; neither shall his place any more behold him.*

Fools try all kinds of fashionable things for happiness. They go from one new thing or method to another. The one thing they will not do is hear the rebuke from the word of God. Oh, that's so yesterday. Who can understand the cryptic Bible? Boring!

Are you tired of happiness that is spotty, bouncy like a yo-yo, and short lived? If so, it is time to examine who you are listening to.

It is better to hear counsels from the word of God. *Proverbs 15:31 The ear that heareth the reproof of life abideth among the wise. Proverbs 1:5 A wise man will hear, and will increase learning; and a man of understanding shall attain unto wise counsels.* God gives mankind the Bible comprised of 66 books (counselors) to direct them in the right paths. Are you taking in and meditating on the word of God daily? *Proverbs 6:20 My son, keep thy father's commandment, and forsake not the law of thy mother: (21) Bind them continually upon thine heart, and tie them about thy neck. (22) When thou goest, it shall lead thee; when thou sleepest, it shall keep thee; and when thou awakest, it shall talk with thee. (23) For the commandment is a lamp; and the law is light; and reproofs of instruction are the way of life.* Read *Proverbs 4, Proverbs 5, Proverbs 15:32, Proverbs 17:10.*

Ecclesiastes 7:7 Surely oppression maketh a wise man mad; and a gift destroyeth the heart. (8) Better is the end of a thing than the beginning thereof: and the patient in spirit is better than the proud in spirit. (9) Be not hasty in thy spirit to be angry: for anger resteth in the bosom of fools. (10) Say not thou, What is the cause that the

former days were better than these? for thou dost not enquire wisely concerning this.

How do you deal with oppression and injustice, and how long can you keep your cool?

Wise people care about justice. Oppressions and briberies in the courts of justice disturb them and tempt them to lose their cool. Some may become angry and call to question God's permissive will in that He would allow such atrocity.

Oppressions and injustices are pervasive in this world. They exist for a number of reasons, chiefly to cause people to despair of this wicked world and to desire the world above the sun through a right relationship with the Son of God. This is not to say we remain passive, hold our tongues, and do nothing to stamp out oppressions and injustices. We should exercise our proper rights, as in voting in good judges and firing the bad ones. The following words of advice help us maintain a proper perspective:

- Check our patience.

  As frequently played out at the end of movies, heroes win and bad guys lose, even though the bad guys initially have the upper hand. The beginning of a thing is just that—the beginning—and we should not presume to know the outcome of an event that is still in motion. When living through oppression, be patient, trust God, and have confidence that He cares and that His truth will prevail in the end, and wickedness will cease. *Psalms 37:34 Wait on the LORD, and keep his way, and he shall exalt thee to inherit the land: when the wicked are cut off, thou shalt see it. (35) I have seen the wicked in great power, and spreading himself like a green bay tree. (36) Yet he passed away, and, lo, he was not: yea, I sought him, but he could not be found. (37) Mark the perfect man, and behold the upright: for the end of that man is* peace. *(38) But the transgressors shall be destroyed together: the end of the wicked shall be cut off. (39) But the salvation of the righteous is of the LORD: he is their strength in the time of trouble. (40) And the LORD shall help them, and deliver them: he shall deliver them from the wicked, and save them, because they trust in him.* Read *Psalms 27:14, Isaiah 40:31.*

- Check our anger.
  This is not to say that we cannot be angry when we are oppressed, but we should not be quick to anger. *James 1:19 Wherefore, my beloved brethren, let every man be swift to hear, slow to speak, slow to wrath: (20) For the wrath of man worketh not the righteousness of God.* As hard as it may be, we must manage our anger, let it pass through, and not allow it to rest and remain in our bosom, for then we will be like the fools. *Ephesians 4:26 Be ye angry, and sin not: let not the sun go down upon your wrath: (27) Neither give place to the devil.* Read *Proverbs 14:17, Proverbs 12:16.*

- Check our complaints.
  We must avoid being righteous in our own eyes as Job, who complained to God about his life adversities and demanded to know the cause of his sufferings. Read *Job 29, Job 30, Job 31.* We should not expect life to be smooth sailing all the way. When in adversity, wrestle not with "Why is this happening to me?" Again, as we learned in *Ecclesiastes 3:1-15,* there is a time and season for everything. In the season of suffering, we are not to inquire why life was better in the good old days or desire to return to those days as the children of Israel did when they wandered in the wilderness of Sin. *Exodus 16:3 And the children of Israel said unto them, Would to God we had died by the hand of the LORD in*

the land of Egypt, when we sat by the flesh pots, and when we did eat bread to the full; for ye have brought us forth into this wilderness, to kill this whole assembly with hunger. We should treat adversities as God working in our lives, refining and shaping us into useful vessels for better days ahead.

Notice the progression: lose our cool, lose control of our anger, and lose our wisdom.

Ecclesiastes 7:11 Wisdom is good with an inheritance: and by it there is profit to them that see the sun. (12) For wisdom is a defence, and money is a defence: but the excellency of knowledge is, that wisdom giveth life to them that have it.

Wisdom is necessary to rightly manage and enjoy an inheritance. To have an inheritance before wisdom is to put the cart before the horse. Many people fantasize having a great estate, but without wisdom, they would be better off not having it. Most people can consume an inheritance—pay off the house, give some money to children and family members, treat them to a nice vacation, and give to charities, but not many people are able to steward and multiply an inheritance. This takes wisdom. (By the way, God gives you a certain number of talents and expects you to steward and multiply them. Read *Matthew 25:14-30*.)

It is a good thing when an inheritance or riches is paired with wisdom. The combination allows the possessors to do much good for themselves, society, and the kingdom of God.

Wisdom protects a person from getting hurt by riches. In a sense, wisdom is a defense, as money is a defense. *Proverbs 18:11 The rich man's wealth is his strong city, and as an high wall in his own conceit.* One can say wisdom is as good as riches. However, wisdom has an important advantage over riches, as riches are unable to protect people from the wrath of God. *Proverbs 11:4 Riches profit not in the day of wrath: but righteousness delivereth from death.*

The life-giving wisdom of God personified in Jesus Christ, according to *1Corinthians 1:24*, protects against the wrath of God. *Romans 10:9 That if thou shalt confess with thy mouth the Lord Jesus, and shalt believe in thine heart that God hath raised him from the dead, <u>thou shalt be saved</u>. (10) For with the heart man believeth unto righteousness; and with the mouth confession is made unto salvation. John 5:24 Verily, verily, I say unto you, He that heareth my word, and believeth on him that sent me, hath everlasting life, and shall not come into condemnation; but is passed from death unto life. 1John 5:12 He that hath the Son hath life; and he that hath not the Son of God hath not life.* Read *Proverbs 3:13-18.*

Imagine what mercy and truth projects you can do for the furtherance of the gospel if you have wisdom and riches.

Ecclesiastes 7:13 Consider the work of God: for who can make that straight, which he hath made crooked? (14) In the day of prosperity be joyful, but in the day of adversity consider: God also hath set the one over against the other, to the end that man should find nothing after him.

Wisdom is necessary for living through evil days when life turns topsy-turvy. It is easy to be cheerful and cocky in good times, but in evil days, will you remain standing when the smoke clears, or will you come undone?

To prepare for and survive the day of adversity, we need to consider the immutability of God's works and our inability to override His will to take charge of our destiny. In other words, if God blesses, who can stop Him? If He makes things crooked (brings about evil days), who can prevent Him?

We need to arm ourselves with the lessons from *Ecclesiastes 3*, because evil days will come. The key to survival is to submit to God's will, be thankful in all circumstances of life, and make the best of every situation. *1Thessalonians 5:18 In every thing give thanks: for this is the will of God in Christ Jesus concerning you.*

In the day of prosperity, be thankful, enjoy it, and serve the Lord with joyfulness and gladness of heart for His abundant provision.

In the day of adversity, be thankful still and regard it as the work of God, for He sets cross events to the intent that mankind should not trust in their circumstances and take things for granted. A Japanese proverb says, "Bad and good are intertwined like rope." We must take the good and the bad.

God is not having fun at our expense. Remember the promises of scripture and learn to appreciate evil days, for there is a purpose for everything, and all will be for the best at last. *Ecclesiastes 3:11a He hath made every thing beautiful in his time.* As we learned in *Ecclesiastes 7:8a* above, *"Better is the end of a thing than the beginning thereof."* Do not waver from serving the Lord. *1Peter 4:12 Beloved, think it not strange concerning the fiery trial which is to try you, as though some strange thing happened unto you: (13) But rejoice, inasmuch as ye are partakers of Christ's sufferings; that, when his glory shall be revealed, ye may be glad also with exceeding joy.*

As Christians who are engaged in spiritual warfare, we need to expect the evil days that come with the territory. Get ready for some pounding from the forces of darkness. If you are taking fire from the evil force for your kingdom work, then praise the Lord, you are on the right track. (You know spiritual warfare is real.) *Ephesians 6:10 Finally, my brethren, be strong in the Lord, and in the power of his might. (11) Put on the whole armour of God, that ye may be able to stand against the wiles of the devil. (12) For we wrestle not against flesh and blood, but against principalities, against powers, against the rulers of the darkness of this world, against spiritual wickedness in high places. (13) Wherefore take unto you the whole armour of God, that ye may be able to withstand in the evil day, and having done all, to stand. (14) Stand therefore, having your loins girt about with truth, and having on the breastplate of righteousness; (15) And your feet shod with the preparation of the gospel of peace; (16) Above all, taking the shield of faith, wherewith ye shall be able to quench all the fiery darts of the wicked. (17) And take the helmet of salvation, and the sword of the Spirit, which is the word of God: (18) Praying always with all prayer and supplication in the Spirit, and watching thereunto with all perseverance and supplication for all saints.*

Will you face your evil days with or without the word of God? Can you recall the promises of scripture when hard times set in?

Ecclesiastes 7:15 All things have I seen in the days of my vanity: there is a just man that perisheth in his righteousness, and there is a wicked man that prolongeth his life in his wickedness. (16) Be not righteous over much; neither make thyself over wise: why shouldest thou destroy thyself? (17) Be not over much wicked, neither be thou foolish: why shouldest thou die before thy time? (18) It is good that thou shouldest take hold of this; yea, also from this withdraw not thine hand: for he that feareth God shall come forth of them all.

Do you have the wisdom to live out your life grant? Suppose God grants you 25,550 days (70 years), do you have the wisdom to live out those days and not die prematurely because of foolish actions?

Solomon observed the two life anomalies noted in verse 15 above. One would think that the opposite is fair—that godly people should live long and wicked people die young. But the passage shows that certain behaviors will destroy people prematurely.

On one extreme is *"a just man that perisheth in his righteousness."* How can this be? (The word "perish" must be understood as the destruction of the physical body as opposed to spiritual damnation of the soul in hell.) Some Christians make themselves spiritual or religious police. Those who assume this role are immature believers who know just enough of the Bible to be stupid and dangerous. They are devoutly religious and make themselves *"righteous over much"* with over-zealousness for their beliefs and a sanctimonious pharisaical attitude. These Bible thumpers constantly judge and find faults in others. They see the mote (straw) in people's eyes, but not the beam in their own eye. Read *Matthew 7:1-5, Luke 18:9-14.* They also like to show themselves *"over wise"* with their irritating know-it-all smart-aleck behavior, meddling in others' affairs. They think they are doing God a favor. These people are not governed by wisdom and make enemies instead of friends. They destroy themselves in their righteousness.

On the other extreme is *"a wicked man that prolongeth his life in his wickedness."* This is because this wicked person is not overly wicked or foolish. He is smart enough to not push his luck too far as to invoke God's judgment early. As such, he gets to live out his life grant. This wicked sinner lives a longer life compared to the unwise *"just man,"* who kills himself with his self-righteousness. (There is a *"sin unto death,"* according to *1John 5:16*, which means certain sin beyond measure will most certainly invoke early judgment and bring about premature death. Case in point, the ISIS executioner Mohammed Emwazi, better known as "Jihadi John," who slit the throats of many innocent people, died at age 27 and is roasting in hell. He now wishes he had never been born.)

The secret to living out our life grant is as follows:

- *"It is good that thou shouldest take hold of this; yea, also from this withdraw not thine hand"*
  We must get a grip on wisdom and not let it go, because it keeps us from getting hurt by extreme, irrational, and foolish behaviors and practices that are *"righteous over much," "over wise,"* and *"over much wicked."* Where does one find wisdom? *Job 28:12-28* is a must read.

- *"For he that feareth God shall come forth of them all"*
  The fear of the Lord is the wisdom that enables individuals to escape the aforementioned extremes. *Proverbs 9:10 The fear of the LORD is the beginning of wisdom: and the knowledge of the holy is understanding. Isaiah 33:6 And wisdom and knowledge shall be the stability of thy times, and strength of salvation: the fear of the LORD is his treasure.* Read *Psalms 111:10, Proverbs 1:7, Proverbs 8:13, Proverbs 10:27.*

Ecclesiastes 7:19 Wisdom strengtheneth the wise more than ten mighty men which are in the city. (20) For there is not a just man upon earth, that doeth good, and sinneth not. (21) Also take no heed unto all words that are spoken; lest thou hear thy servant curse thee: (22) For oftentimes also thine own heart knoweth that thou thyself likewise hast cursed others.

Do you expect your pastors, ministry leaders, or friends to be faultless? Have you ever been hurt by or disappointed in them? Their behaviors, sins, or offenses may have injured you emotionally with the pain penetrating so deep in your soul that you resent them. Do you have the instructions of wisdom for coping with such emotional bumps and bruises?

Wisdom strengthens the inner person, providing stay and support. Read *Ephesians 3:13-16*. Continuing with the idea of wisdom as a defense from *Ecclesiastes 12a*, here it says that a person who possesses and uses wisdom is stronger than 10 mighty men who guard a city. The word "strengthen" is also translated as "prevail," in that wisdom prevails over the muscles of flesh. *Proverbs 21:22 A wise man scaleth the city of the mighty, and casteth down the strength of the confidence thereof. Proverbs 24:5 A wise man is strong; yea, a man of knowledge increaseth strength.*

Wisdom strengthens us to forgive and teaches us not to expect flawlessness in people. No one is perfect or sinless, not even the *"just man"* who is full of good works. To err is human. (Now, if the offense is a criminal act, then we need to go a step further and refer it to the authorities.)

Since no one is perfect, wisdom also teaches us to pay no attention to the sentiments of the people who work closely with us, like coworkers and peers. The daily interaction can sometimes create friction and annoyances that, if we listen in on their conversations or monitor their chat rooms, we may hear them degrading us, which may then trigger a reactive resentment in us. But truth be told, we ourselves have often degraded others. We must simply accept the fact that people will talk behind our backs and not be moved by the things that are said of us. Good words feed pride; ill words stir up passion.

It is better to be strengthened by wisdom than by the flesh, because we fight our demons daily, and the battle is psychological, spiritual, and emotional in nature. *Ephesians 6:12 For we wrestle not against flesh and blood, but against principalities, against powers, against the rulers of the darkness of this world, against spiritual wickedness in high places.* The power of the flesh is of little use in spiritual warfare. *1Timothy 4:8a For bodily exercise profiteth little.* Wisdom keeps us on solid footing, emotionally stable, rational, sensible, away from the aforementioned extremes, and strengthens us to perform our duties to God under sufferings. No one is free from sin and its downfall. When we sin, wisdom helps us to repent and bounce back, restoring fellowship with God. *Proverbs 24:16 For a just man falleth seven times, and riseth up again: but the wicked shall fall into mischief.*

If you do not have the wisdom of God, you do not have the inner strength to defend against sin and spiritual attacks. (Godly wisdom has a spiritual component to it.) You will have to rely on the strength of your flesh as the *"mighty men."* But flesh can only sin and take you down hurtful paths. *Galatians 5:9 Now the works of the flesh are manifest, which are these; Adultery, fornication, uncleanness, lasciviousness, (20) Idolatry, witchcraft, hatred, variance, emulations, wrath, strife, seditions, heresies, (21) Envyings, murders, drunkenness, revellings, and such like: of the which I tell you before, as I have also told you in time past, that they which do such things shall not inherit the kingdom of God.*

Ecclesiastes 7:23 All this have I proved by wisdom: I said, I will be wise; but it was far from me. (24) That which is far off, and exceeding deep, who can find it out? (25) I applied mine heart to know, and to search, and to seek out wisdom, and the reason of things, and to know the wickedness of folly, even of foolishness and madness: (26) And I find more bitter than death the woman, whose heart is snares and nets, and her hands as bands: whoso pleaseth God shall escape from her; but the sinner shall be taken by her.

God gave Solomon an extraordinary capacity for knowledge and discernment above any. Even so, Solomon admitted that there was knowledge so far and deep beyond his reach and comprehension. *Job 11:7 Canst thou by searching find out God? canst thou find out the Almighty unto perfection? (8) It is as high as heaven; what canst thou do? deeper than hell; what canst thou know? (9) The measure thereof is longer than the earth, and broader than the sea. Romans 11:33 O the depth of the riches both of the wisdom and knowledge of God! how unsearchable are his judgments, and his ways past finding out!* A Japanese proverb says, "If you understand everything, you must be misinformed."

With his wisdom and pricey experience, Solomon was able to unveil the disguise of vanity and prove that this world has nothing to make a person happy. It was a pricey experience because he went to the dark side with his experiments. He wanted to know what humans, apart from God, could do to be happy in this world, both in the works of wisdom and folly (*Ecclesiastes 1:13*). He was not satisfied by mere concept, theory, or logic, but desired considerable empirical evidence for the nature and *"the reason of things."* He was studious, applying his heart to serious learning. He was not discouraged by the difficult task, but was provoked to undertake it. He painstakingly pried into and made trial of *"all things that are done under heaven."* (Review the "Vanity of Knowledge" and "Vanity of Worldly Pleasures and Possessions" chapters.)

When he indulged in madness and folly (*Ecclesiastes 1:17*), he went all out, desiring to know and taste the *"wickedness of folly, even of foolishness and madness."* Of all his sinful follies, there was one in particular that got him good and weighed heavily upon his conscience—the marrying of ungodly women—a sin that he said was *"more bitter than death."* *1Kings 11:1 But king Solomon loved many strange women, together with the daughter of Pharaoh, women of the Moabites, Ammonites, Edomites, Zidonians, and Hittites; (2) Of the nations concerning which the LORD said unto the children of Israel, Ye shall not go in to them, neither shall they come in unto you: for surely they will turn away your heart after their gods: Solomon clave unto these in love. (3) And he had seven hundred wives, princesses, and three hundred concubines: and his wives turned away his heart.*

Solomon lamented that he was drawn away from God and became a pagan idolater by *"the woman, whose heart is snares and nets, and her hands as bands."* He probably initially thought they were marriages made in heaven, but to his nightmare, they were marriages made in hell. *1Kings 11:4 For it came to pass, when Solomon was old, that his wives turned away his heart after other gods: and his heart was not perfect with the LORD his God, as was the heart of David his father. (5) For Solomon went after Ashtoreth the goddess of the Zidonians, and after Milcom the abomination of the Ammonites. (6) And Solomon did evil in the sight of the LORD, and went not fully after the LORD, as did David his father. (7) Then did Solomon build an high place for Chemosh, the abomination of Moab, in the hill that is before Jerusalem, and for Molech, the abomination of the children of Ammon. (8) And likewise did he for all his strange wives, which burnt incense and sacrificed unto their gods.* (The worship of Molech involved the abominable human sacrifice of children by fire. Read *Leviticus 18:21, Leviticus 20:1-5.*)

Solomon went on to describe the clever disguise of the sin that ruined him. It was snares, nets, and bands (SNB) packaged in the bodies of beautiful and sexy women. The attraction and seduction were so strong that only those who pleased God could escape the temptation. Sinners would definitely be caught in the trap.

Think of Potiphar's wife. I am pretty sure she put on a show when she seduced Joseph. Read *Genesis 39:7-12.* I am willing to bet that she didn't entice Joseph in a T-shirt and blue jeans. Good for Joseph; he saw a sexy SNB coming and went straight for the door.

Think of Delilah. Was she not the queen of SNB? She essentially applied Chinese water torture on Samson and eventually ruined him. *Judges 16:15 And she said unto him, How canst thou say, I love thee, when thine heart is not with me? thou hast mocked me these three times, and hast not told me wherein thy great strength lieth. (16) And it came to pass, when she pressed him daily* with her words, and urged him, so that his soul was vexed unto death. Read *Judges 16* for the full story.

God has repeatedly warned His children not to marry unbelievers, both in the Old and New Testament. *2Corinthians 6:14 Be ye not unequally yoked together with unbelievers: for what fellowship hath righteousness with unrighteousness? and what communion hath light with darkness? (15) And what concord hath Christ with Belial? or what part hath he that believeth with an infidel? (16) And what agreement hath the temple of God with idols? for ye are the temple of the living God; as God hath said, I will dwell in them, and walk in them; and I will be their God, and they shall be my people.* Read *Genesis 24:3-4.*

If you don't have the fear of God and don't live His words, chances are you will end up marrying an SNB, because you will walk after your heart and the lusts of your eyes. Snares, nets, and bands put you in bondage, take you out of fellowship, and eventually ruin you. You will regret the decision and agree with *Proverbs 5:12-13*, *"How have I hated instruction, and my heart despised reproof; And have not obeyed the voice of my teachers, nor inclined mine ear to them that instructed me!"*

You should not marry an SNB, neither should you give your sons and daughters to them. SNBs are MBD (*"more bitter than death"*).

Ecclesiastes 7:27 Behold, this have I found, saith the preacher, counting one by one, to find out the account: (28) Which yet my soul seeketh, but I find not: one man among a thousand have I found; but a woman among all those have I not found. (29) Lo, this only have I found, that God hath made man upright; but they have sought out many inventions.

Another lesson Solomon learned from his sin, besides the fact that it was *"more bitter than death,"* was that it was also dissatisfying—*"Which yet my soul seeketh, but I find not."* As he recalled and counted each and every intimate experience and relationship with the ungodly women, he found that while they were the desire of his flesh, they were not the kind that his soul longed for, which was a virtuous and upright woman. Such a woman doesn't exist among ungodly ladies. He expressed it idiomatically as *"one man among a thousand have I found; but a woman among all those have I not found."* Read *Proverbs 31:10*. The reason is that God made *"man"* (Adam) upright, but since his fall, *"they"* (Adam and his offspring) invented all kinds of contrarian ways for righteousness, wisdom, and happiness. *Proverbs 18:1 Through desire a man, having separated himself, seeketh and intermeddleth with all wisdom.*

We live in a time of rapid moral degeneration. We don't see evil for what it is. Our society glamorizes evil, calling evil good and good evil. People make light of sin and *"draw iniquity with cords of vanity, and sin as it were with a cart rope."* Read *Isaiah 5:18-23.* There is wickedness in folly. Solomon's research included the knowledge of the *"wickedness of folly, even of foolishness and madness."* To dabble in folly is to dabble in wickedness. People think innocent folly is fun, not realizing it is the façade of wickedness and the gateway to deadlier sins. For example, recreational use of cannabis may be legal in some states, but it is a gateway to stronger stuff. If you dabble in this, you will open a new life chapter—"Voyage to the bottom."

Sex outside of marriage is easier than ever with the plethora of hookup apps. To get laid, simply swipe right. Like Solomon, one of these days, these sinners will find themselves in snares, nets, and bands, and the whole experience is *"more bitter than death."* One of the sins will destroy them no matter how smart and careful they are. *Numbers 32:23b* says, *"Be sure your sin will find you out."* *Galatians 6:7 Be not deceived; God is not mocked: for whatsoever a man soweth, that shall he also reap.* Please heed God's warnings. *Proverbs 5* is a must read.

Doctrinally, the woman in *Ecclesiastes 7:26* is a type of religion. Read *Proverbs 7* and replace the *"woman with the attire of an harlot"* with religion and you will see how religion draws people in, puts them in bondage, and kills them. It has been said that religion sends more people to hell than all the vices combined. To be right with God, replace religion with a right relationship with His Son, Jesus Christ.

The man in the idiom *"one man among a thousand have I found; but a woman among all those have I not found"* prophetically points to the Lord Jesus Christ, as He is the only sinless, righteous, virtuous, and upright God-man.

Final Thoughts

Wisdom is required for living a meaningful and fulfilled life. *Proverbs 4:5 Get wisdom, get understanding: forget it not; neither decline from the words of my mouth. (6) Forsake her not, and she shall preserve thee: love her, and she shall keep thee. (7) Wisdom is the principal thing; therefore get wisdom: and with all thy getting get understanding. (8) Exalt her, and she shall promote thee: she shall bring thee to honour, when thou dost embrace her. (9) She shall give to thine head an ornament of grace: a crown of glory shall she deliver to thee.*

Wisdom comes from God's word and is personified in Jesus Christ. *Proverbs 2:6 For the LORD giveth wisdom: out of his mouth cometh knowledge and understanding. (7) He layeth up sound wisdom for the righteous: he is a buckler to them that walk uprightly.* Read *Proverbs 2, 1Corinthians 1:24*. Fools, however, despise wisdom and instruction. No Jesus, no wisdom; know Jesus, know wisdom. It doesn't work to approach the Bible academically without a personal relationship with Jesus Christ. The Bible is a spiritual book that is mysterious and cryptic to natural-born people, but it is magical with infinite depth to those who are born again and illuminated by the Holy Spirit of God. *1Corinthians 2:14 But the natural man receiveth not the things of the Spirit of God: for they are foolishness unto him: neither can he know them, because they are spiritually discerned.*

God would love for you to have His wisdom. *James 1:5 If any of you lack wisdom, let him ask of God, that giveth to all men liberally, and upbraideth not; and it shall be given him. (6) But let him ask in faith, nothing wavering. For he that wavereth is like a wave of the sea driven with the wind and tossed.* How much wisdom you get is up to you. As the saying goes, "You get out of life what you put into it," so dig into the Bible, learn the instructions of wisdom, and use them in your life. May God teach you in the way of wisdom and lead you in right paths.

13 – Happiness is in This Relationship

"I would be the happiest person in the world if you would marry me. Baby, you complete me." Sound familiar? So the holy grail of your happiness is in a person of your type, who is as flawed as you?

Tired of unhappy relationships? It's time to examine your relationship with the King of Kings. Featured herein are seven essential qualities for maintaining a healthy relationship with the King of Kings:

1. Wise people keep the King's commandments – *Ecclesiastes 8:2*.
2. Wise people abide in the word of the King – *Ecclesiastes 8:3*.
3. Wise people recognize the awesome power of the word of the King – *Ecclesiastes 8:4*.
4. Wise people do the right thing at the right time according to the word of the King – *Ecclesiastes 8:5*.
5. Wise people don't procrastinate in their duty to the King – *Ecclesiastes 8:6-8*.
6. Wise people thrive and are fruitful under the tyrannical rule of earthly kings – *Ecclesiastes 8:9-13*.
7. Wise people serve the King without wavering, even when bad things happen to them – *Ecclesiastes 8:14-17*.

Ecclesiastes 8:1 Who is as the wise man? and who knoweth the interpretation of a thing? a man's wisdom maketh his face to shine, and the boldness of his face shall be changed.

A wise person is to be appreciated and praised—*"Who is as the wise man?"* Compare this to the praise of God. *Exodus 15:11 Who is like unto thee, O LORD, among the gods? who is like thee, glorious in holiness, fearful in praises, doing wonders?* The answer is no one. Likewise, a wise person who knows the right and godly interpretation of things, teaches aright from God's truths, and conveys godly solutions—*"Thus saith the LORD"*—for difficult issues has no compeer. In other words, "You're the man!" As *"wisdom excelleth folly, as far as light excelleth darkness (Ecclesiastes 2:13),"* a wise person also excels others.

We can spot a person who is governed by wisdom—*"a man's wisdom maketh his face to shine, and the boldness of his face shall be changed."* Wisdom transfigures the countenance with a look that shouts godliness. Moses had a radiating aura when he came down from the mountain after spending 40 days with God. Stephen's wisdom was undisputable, and his debaters saw his face as if it was the face of an angel. Read *Exodus 34:27-35, Acts 6:8-15, Acts 4:13.* Wisdom alters a person's countenance from a fierce, defiant, and proud demeanor, to a soft, gentle, meek, and loving countenance. A wise person is very approachable. One shouldn't be afraid to come to a wise person with Bible questions. Conversely, *"a wicked man hardeneth his face,"* according to *Proverbs 21:29a.*

It is important to note that the mark of wisdom is not head knowledge or the outward appearance, because nothing but a complete change of heart can benefit a person. The face reflects the work of the Holy Spirit in the heart. He opens spiritual eyes and gives understanding and insight into God's truth. Wisdom results when a person responds with obedience and faithfulness to God's commandments, as in verses 2 and 3 below.

Ecclesiastes 8:2 I counsel thee to keep the king's commandment, and that in regard of the oath of God.

To keep a commandment (the oath or word of God) is to obey. Wise people differentiate themselves by obeying the word of God. They know the word is not only true, but truth by which they obtain salvation, a clear perspective of the world, the will of God concerning them, and instructions for living a meaningful and happy life. To them, the word of God is more precious than gold and is profitable for all aspects of the Christian life. *2Timothy 3:15 And that from a child thou hast known the holy scriptures, which are able to make thee wise unto salvation through faith which is in Christ Jesus. (16) All scripture is given by inspiration of God, and is profitable for doctrine, for reproof, for correction, for instruction in righteousness: (17) That the man of God may be perfect, throughly furnished unto all good works.* Read *Proverbs 3:1-26, Proverbs 4, Proverbs 5, Proverbs 6:20-35, Proverbs 7:1-5, Proverbs 8:32-36.*

Can one obey God's commandments and not know the Bible? If God's wisdom is in His word, can one be wise without knowing the Bible?

There is no getting around learning the Bible if we are to be wise. Sadly, many Christians are perfectly content with light Bible reading for its stories, especially stories on how much God loves them. We must graduate from picture book to chapter book, from stories to doctrines, or as the Apostle Paul puts it, from milk to meat (*1Corinthians 3:2, Hebrews 5:12*). The treasures of the sea are at the bottom of the ocean, and we cannot get to them by snorkeling in the shallows. Likewise, the treasures of wisdom and knowledge of God are hidden in Christ (*Colossians 2:3*), and we will not attain unto wise counsels without an intimate knowledge of the Bible.

Until we recognize our desperate need for and accountability to the word of God, we will remain as shallow

Christians in a tide pool complaining that the ocean is not deep enough. We will not achieve spiritual maturity if we are unable to feed ourselves the word of God. We will live according to the world, being tossed to and fro, and carried about with every wind of doctrine.

Learning the Bible is hard, there is no sugarcoating it. Much effort is required. *Proverbs 2:1 My son, if thou wilt receive my words, and hide my commandments with thee; (2) So that thou incline thine ear unto wisdom, and apply thine heart to understanding; (3) Yea, if thou criest after knowledge, and liftest up thy voice for understanding; (4) If thou seekest her as silver, and searchest for her as for hid treasures; (5) Then shalt thou understand the fear of the LORD, and find the knowledge of God.*

- There is a price to pay for truth. The phrase *"I counsel thee"* appears only twice in the Bible. The other time is in *Revelation 3:18, "I counsel thee to buy of me gold tried in the fire, that thou mayest be rich; and white raiment, that thou mayest be clothed, and that the shame of thy nakedness do not appear; and anoint thine eyes with eyesalve, that thou mayest see."*

- As with the acquisition of any knowledge, it takes great discipline and effort to learn the Bible. Unlike any other knowledge, virtue is a prerequisite for spiritual knowledge. *2Peter 1:5 And beside this, giving all diligence, add to your faith virtue; and to virtue knowledge.* A wicked person can learn and understand science, but not the Bible.

- The difficulty of learning is compounded by our flesh, which loves to procrastinate and has a natural tendency to despise and disobey truth.

- The devil will do everything to keep us from knowing truth and being useful to God. We pick up the Bible and suddenly find reasons to put it away. The devil will, however, allow us to spend excessive amounts of time pursuing activities that have no spiritual value. We must break free from our couch's gravitational pull and study the Bible rather than binging on TV programs.

Just when we think we are ready to learn the Bible, here is a bucket of cold water. Living the Bible is much harder than learning it. This is where the rubber meets the road. It is not easy to live a faithful and blameless (not sinless) life surrounded by temptations. We must carry our cross and die to self daily, making good judgment calls for every temptation that presents itself. *Galatians 5:16 This I say then, Walk in the Spirit, and ye shall not fulfil the lust of the flesh.* The choices are the Via Dolorosa path of truth that leads to joy or the self-serving street of vanity that leads to emptiness, misery, depression, and death. As salmons swim upstream, battling strong currents and risking being caught by bears and fishermen in order to spawn and fulfill their calling, so must we with courage and wisdom, live out God's truth in our lives. This brings us to the second distinguishing quality of wise people— abiding.

Ecclesiastes 8:3 Be not hasty to go out of his sight: stand not in an evil thing; for he doeth whatsoever pleaseth him.

We live in a highly charged PC (politically correct) society. People's fuses are not only short, they are already lit. People are easily offended.

Wise people are not offended by the hard sayings in the Bible. They abide and are not *"hasty to go out of his sight,"* as in to depart from faith. Consider Jesus' discourse in *John 6* where He presented Himself as the Bread of Life to the Jews in a synagogue in

Capernaum. At one point in the discourse He said, *"Verily, verily, I say unto you, Except ye eat the flesh of the Son of man, and drink his blood, ye have no life in you. Whoso eateth my flesh, and drinketh my blood, hath eternal life; and I will raise him up at the last day. For my flesh is meat indeed, and my blood is drink indeed. He that eateth my flesh, and drinketh my blood, dwelleth in me, and I in him. As the living Father hath sent me, and I live by the Father: so he that eateth me, even he shall live by me. This is that bread which came down from heaven: not as your fathers did eat manna, and are dead: he that eateth of this bread shall live for ever."* (John 6:53-58) The sayings were too gruesome and offensive to some disciples, who said, *"This is an hard saying; who can hear it?"* Subsequently, many left Jesus and went their own way. *John 6:66 From that time many of his disciples went back, and walked no more with him.* (Interesting chapter and verse numbers: 6:66.) God doesn't care about political correctness; He cares about truth.

People who are not anchored in the word of God are prone to be offended by the trials of their faith. These people are portrayed in the Parable of the Sower in *Matthew 13* as those who *"received the seed in stony places." Matthew 13:20 But he that received the seed into stony places, the same is he that heareth the word, and anon with joy receiveth it; (21) Yet hath he not root in himself, but dureth for a while: for when tribulation or persecution ariseth because of the word, by and by he is offended.* They love the message of salvation and the forgiveness of sins and accept Jesus Christ for the good life. And because their knowledge of the word of God is as shallow as the dirt in stony places, they fail miserably when their faith is tested, and say, "This Jesus thing is not working for me." (By the way, the Bible never promises a good life. Instead, it promises sufferings and a meaningful life. The believers in Thessalonica were praised by the Apostle Paul for their faith that withstood persecutions. They received the word of God in much affliction, with joy of the Holy Ghost.) Read the Parable of the Sower in *Matthew 13:1-23* and ask yourself which person you are in the story. Also read *1Thessalonians* chapters 1 thru 3.

Jesus said in *Matthew 11:6, "And blessed* (happy) *is he, whosoever shall not be offended in me."*

People who depart from their faith in Jesus Christ return to the devil they know and their old sinful lifestyle. Hence *Ecclesiastes8:3a* says, *"Be not hasty to go out of his sight: stand not in an evil thing,"* because God is terrible (not in the awful sense, but dreadful). He can tear a person up; He can inflict whatever punishment He sees fit on sinners. *Psalms 115:3 But our God is in the heavens: he hath done whatsoever he hath pleased.*

Ecclesiastes 8:4 Where the word of a king is, there is power: and who may say unto him, What doest thou?

Another reason why wise people keep the King's commandments is because of the great power of His word. His word goes forth with power to accomplish His will, and not one jot of the word will fail. His promises are sure and He will make good on His threats, which is a force to be reckoned with. Those in their right minds would never dare to challenge His words or call Him to account for His acts. *Isaiah 55:11 So shall my word be that goeth forth out of my mouth: it shall not return unto me void, but it shall accomplish that which I please, and it shall prosper in the thing whereto I sent it.* Read *Hebrews 4:12, Psalms 33:8, Psalms 29:4, Luke 12:4-5, Luke 4:31-36, Luke 8:22-25, Matthew 5:18.*

Wise people lay to heart the awesome power of the word of God, the authority that goes with it, and the consequences of rebelling against it. The Bible is the wise person's final authority resulting in fear, respect, and obedience to the word.

Skeptics like to discredit the power and authority of the word of God by arguing that the Bible is human literature. I challenge these people to choose any of God's commandments and do the exact opposite, and see how life works out for them. No one can violate the word of God and succeed. There is power in the word.

Only a being with an infinite mind who lives outside of time and space could have written the Bible. The word is given to mankind by inspiration. *2Timothy 3:16 All scripture is given by inspiration of God, and is profitable for doctrine, for reproof, for correction, for instruction in righteousness.* We should not pretend to know God if we do not know the Bible. Our relationship with God is as good as our obedience to His word.

What's your plan for learning the Bible?

Ecclesiastes 8:5 Whoso keepeth the commandment shall feel no evil thing: and a wise man's heart discerneth both time and judgment.

Wise people know the King's commandments (the Bible), and having settled in their hearts concerning the power of His word, they perform their duties in a proper manner and season. As such, they avoid the dreadful sentence of judgment that befalls delinquents and the rebellious. *Proverbs 12:21 There shall no evil happen to the just: but the wicked shall be filled with mischief.*

Every Christian should know that God expects His children to love one another and to co-labor with Him in kingdom work, which includes evangelism and discipleship. *John 14:12 Verily, verily, I say unto you, He that believeth on me, the works that I do shall he do also; and greater works than these shall he do; because I go unto my Father.* The proper time to perform the works is now. Enough time has been wasted. *Ephesians 5:16 Redeeming the time, because the days are evil.* Don't be unwise in delaying to perform these duties.

Ecclesiastes 8:6 Because to every purpose there is time and judgment, therefore the misery of man is great upon him. (7) For he knoweth not that which shall be: for who can tell him when it shall be? (8) There is no man that hath power over the spirit to retain the spirit; neither hath he power in the day of death: and there is no discharge in that war; neither shall wickedness deliver those that are given to it.

Every individual's life events are determined and appointed by God and are concealed. No one knows what will happen next or when it will happen. Being in the dark concerning the future, with no ability to influence the course, brings great misery upon mankind. When people have no foresight of bad events, they cannot avoid or guard against them. They are always in reactive mode.

Even the wise are blindsided by many things, including the day of death.

How much influence and power do people have over death? Let us count the ways.

1. *"There is no man that hath power over the spirit to retain the spirit"* – The human spirit is the energy of life. It belongs to God and is on loan from Him. If God recalls the spirit, the individual has no power to retain it.

2. *"Neither hath he power in the day of death"* – God determines the day of death for every person, and no one has the power to prevent or postpone it.

3. *"And there is no discharge in that war"* – In the war with death, humans are locked in the no-win fatal conflict with no ability to dismiss or discharge themselves.

4. *"Neither shall wickedness deliver those that are given to it"* – Though a wicked person may live a long life, wickedness itself has no inherent power to deliver from death. *Proverbs 11:4 Riches profit not in the day of wrath: but righteousness delivereth from death.*

Under these circumstances, wise individuals will not procrastinate in accomplishing what is expected of them by the King. They make hay while the sun shines, because there is no guarantee of tomorrow.

Pause to consider what you have to show at the Judgment Seat of Christ if you were to die today.

Ecclesiastes 8:9 All this have I seen, and applied my heart unto every work that is done under the sun: there is a time wherein one man ruleth over another to his own hurt. (10) And so I saw the wicked buried, who had come and gone from the place of the holy, and they were forgotten in the city where they had so done: this is also vanity. (11) Because sentence against an evil work is not executed speedily, therefore the heart of the sons of men is fully set in them to do evil. (12) Though a sinner do evil an hundred times, and his days be prolonged, yet surely I know that it shall be well with them that fear God, which fear before him: (13) But it shall not be well with the wicked, neither shall he prolong his days, which are as a shadow; because he feareth not before God.

Here is yet an anomaly and sadness under the sun and another reason for not liking this world.

There are wicked rulers who seek happiness in power and evil works and are not punished for their wickedness. They sit in judgment in the courts of judicature while they brutally oppress their subjects. *Proverbs 28:15 As a roaring lion, and a ranging bear; so is a wicked ruler over the poor people.* They prosper in the abuse of power, and their days are also prolonged. In the end, they die and are buried and forgotten, just like everyone else in this world.

"Because sentence against an evil work is not executed speedily," these wicked rulers deceive themselves. Their prosperity emboldens and hardens them in their wickedness. Their hearts are fully set to do evil. They think God is asleep at the switch. They get away with an inch and keep pushing. So the world is increasingly evil.

Naïve people expect a moral human government and swift judgment on sinners. They cannot comprehend why the wicked prosper in their ways and why God hasn't mopped up the injustices in this world. Some even resort to protesting, rioting, and taking the law into their own hands. But wise people who know the Bible know for certain that even though judgment comes slowly, it comes surely. The Judgment Seat of Christ awaits Christians, while the Great White Throne judgment is reserved for unbelievers. Read *2Corinthians 5:10, Revelation 20:11-15. Matthew 12:36 But I say unto you, That every idle word that men shall speak, they shall give account thereof in the day of judgment. (37) For by thy words thou shalt be justified, and by thy words thou shalt be condemned.*

    a) It shall be well with those who do not envy or go in the way of the wicked. The presence of God in their hearts keeps them in the fear of the Almighty and away from sin. *Proverbs 24:1 Be not thou envious against evil men, neither desire to be with them. Psalms 1:1 Blessed is the man that walketh not in the counsel of the ungodly, nor standeth in the way of sinners, nor sitteth in the seat of the scornful. (2) But his delight is in the law of the LORD; and in his law doth he meditate day and night.*

    b) It shall not be well with the wicked, even though *"a sinner do evil an hundred times, and his days be prolonged."* Yet their days on earth are as a shadow, *empty, and worthless. Psalms 144:4 Man is like to vanity: his days are as a shadow that passeth away. Hebrews 9:27 And as it is appointed unto men once to die, but after this the judgment.*

The godly in adversity is better than the wicked in prosperity. It's real simple; if God is true, then all sinners are in trouble, no matter how often they get away with their wickedness. Every sin will be judged and punished. Every transgression and disobedience shall receive a just retribution. Evil days and the oppressions of the wicked do not shake wise people's faith in God's word. They leave the retributive justice to God. *Romans 12:19 Dearly beloved, avenge not yourselves, but rather give place unto wrath: for it is written, Vengeance is mine; I will repay, saith the Lord.* Wise people can thrive under tyrannical rule and still manage to be fruitful for God by practicing *Romans 13:1-7, Titus 3:1-2, 1Peter 2:13-17.*

(Tranquility is the essence of happiness, and submission is necessary for a tranquil life. Wise people understand this prudent view of life and obey their authorities. As Christians, we must understand the Biblical context of submission to human authority. We are to obey the government, however bad it may be, but whenever there is a conflict with scripture, we are to obey the highest power—God. *Acts 5:29 Then Peter and the other apostles answered and said, We ought to obey God rather than men.*)

Ecclesiastes 8:14 There is a vanity which is done upon the earth; that there be just men, unto whom it happeneth according to the work of the wicked; again, there be wicked men, to whom it happeneth according to the work of the righteous: I said that this also is vanity. (15) Then I commended mirth, because a man hath no better thing under the sun, than to eat, and to drink, and to be merry: for that shall abide with him of his labour the days of his life, which God giveth him under the sun. (16) When I applied mine heart to know wisdom, and to see the business that is done upon the earth: (for also there is that neither day nor night seeth sleep with his eyes:) (17) Then I beheld all the work of God, that a man cannot find out the work that is done under the sun: because though a man labour to seek it out, yet he shall not find it; yea further; though a wise man think to know it, yet shall he not be able to find it.

Something strange is happening in this world. There is a particular unreasonable vanity in which the distribution of good and evil seems dysfunctional, in that bad things happen to good people, and good things happen to bad people. Those without understanding are mad at God over this anomaly.

This anomaly is by God's design so that humans do not place their hopes in this world, because life is uncertain, and they are not in charge of their destiny.

People who have no hope beyond this life have no choice but to be fond of this messed up world, as this is the closest they will ever get to heaven. Upon this consideration, there is no better thing than for them to live out their fleeting and meaningless life by living for the present, entertaining themselves with the fruit of their labor—eating, drinking, and being merry. With the inability to take anything with them in death, their best course is to enjoy what they have now. This enjoyment is a gift from God, to be earned by labor and received with thanksgiving. It is the closest they will ever come to happiness.

Unfortunately, these self-serving people are not smart enough. Instead of comfortably enjoying their remaining days, which is their best advantage, they work incessantly through a hive of human industry trying to secure their destiny against God's providence. It is a futile effort, because no one knows how the mystery of God's inscrutable dealings with the just and wicked works. (Before one can fix something, one must know how it works.) It is beyond the reach of human labor—*"though a man labour to seek it out, yet he shall not find it,"* and the grasp of human wisdom—*"though a wise man think to know it, yet shall he not be able to find it." Romans 11:33 O the depth of the riches both of the wisdom and knowledge of God! how unsearchable are his judgments, and his ways past finding out!* It is unfortunate that these people will not submit to God's will and providence, but busy themselves to prevent unpreventable life events, as we learned in Chapter 7.

Smart servants of God do not perplex themselves with this anomaly or fear future events that are beyond their control. They continue to live a meaningful life by serving God without wavering when bad things happen to them.

Note:

A meaningful life is spiritual and is measured by one's service to the Lord, powered by the Spirit of God, whereas a good life is typically measured by one's worldly achievements and possessions, powered by money. In my native Asian culture, men's idea of a good life is having a ton of money, and ladies' idea of a good life is having a loving husband, raising a "mommy's boy" son, and having money. God is someone they worship for the good life. (Heck, they will worship anything that promises them a good life. Some even go to the graveyard to worship ghosts to receive lottery numbers.)

In many parts of the world, the common thinking is, "Let me first have a good life, then I will serve God," or "When I get this, then I will serve." In other words, let me first serve the gods of stuff, and then I will serve the real God with my leftovers. Think about that logic for a moment. Do you think the strategy will work out well? *Exodus 20:3 Thou shalt have no other gods before me.*

I am not against people having and living a good life. Who doesn't want that? Even a dog wants it. The point is, it never works to prioritize self before God. A life that is worldly rich and spiritually bankrupt is vanity.

It takes a lot of money to have the good life advertised by the world. Big money is out of reach for most people. Yet there is no lack of hopefuls who are hooked on the prospect of being rich, and in the meantime enslaving themselves to the mighty dollar. *Luke 16:13 No servant can serve two masters: for either he will hate the one, and love the other; or else he will hold to the one, and despise the other. Ye cannot serve God and mammon.* On the flip side, anyone can live a meaningful life by serving God.

About this time, some might ask, "Is it possible to strike a balance—be successful in the world and have a healthy spiritual life?" Yes, many God-loving Christians juggle work and ministry. They have a right priority, viewing their income as a means to further the gospel. In terms of balance, conceptually, one attempts to maintain a 50-50 work-ministry balance, but in practice, the course is always lopsided, like a ship listing back and forth toward the port and starboard, with a constant need to right the ship. Their love for God and His kingdom helps them to rebalance. Maintaining a balance also requires sacrifices. Are you willing to part with the things that you really want and use the money in ministry instead? How easy is it for you to part with the good life if God asks you to suffer for Him? *Matthew 19:16-24* talks about a rich young man who was ready to follow Jesus after acquiring much worldly goods. How successful was he in following Jesus?

Final Thoughts

What do ants and acacia trees, clownfish and sea anemones, and dogs and humans have in common? They have symbiotic relationships in which both parties benefit, and many of these relationships are long-lasting. What type of relationship do you have with God?

God has called Christians to salvation and service, but many opt for the good life and abuse His grace by taking the ticket to heaven and dropping the service. Read *2Corinthians 5:17-18*. The worldly Christianity of today is about living well, being satisfied by the things of the world, and seeing their children grow up and have good jobs. Wait... don't unsaved people also have the same goals? The Apostle Paul counted all his possessions as dung (*Philippians 3:8*). In service to the Lord, he was whipped five times, each with 39 flesh-tearing lashes, and beaten with rods (picture baseball bats) three times for sharing the good news of salvation. This was just the tip of the iceberg of his sufferings. How many bones were broken and re-broken in his body? Do you think he walked upright after that? Countless others have suffered and given their all for the cause of Christ. "The Trail of Blood," "Foxe's Book of Martyrs," and "Giants of the Missionary Trail" are some of the books that every Christian should read. These people did not live a good life by the world's standards, but they lived a meaningful and joyful life. Do people like these still exist? Yes! You should subscribe to "The Voice of the Martyrs" at https://www.persecution.com. *2Timothy 3:12 Yea, and all that will live godly in Christ Jesus shall suffer persecution.*

If you want to go to heaven but are living for self, you don't understand salvation. Salvation is a transaction—your life in exchange for the forgiveness of sin. Jesus Christ owns you. A parasitic relationship guarantees unhappiness.

Are you a threat to the devil? If you are not sharing the gospel and discipling people in the word of God, you are not doing God a service, and the devil will leave you alone to enjoy your good life in vanity. *2Timothy 2:4 No man that warreth entangleth himself with the affairs of this life; that he may please him who hath chosen him to be a soldier.* If you have a genuine encounter with God, you will be like Isaiah in *Isaiah 6*. First, you will realize what a sinner you are—*"Woe is me! for I am undone; because I am a man of unclean lips, and I dwell in the midst of a people of unclean lips: for mine eyes have seen the King, the LORD of hosts."* Second, you will realize what an incredible salvation God has provided through Jesus Christ—*"Thine iniquity is taken away, and thy sin purged."* Third, you will realize that God saved you on purpose for a great purpose, and you will hear the call and get to work—*"Whom shall I send, and who will go for us? Then said I, Here am I; send me."*

Happiness is in a right relationship with the King of Kings. May God mold you into a profitable servant and soldier of Christ to live a meaningful life.

14 – Living with Divine Providence

L ife is a bowl of cherries once you accept Jesus Christ as Lord and Savior, right? No, people are mad at God for the anomalies in this world. Good things happen to bad people; bad things happen to good people; oppressions and injustices abound; the wicked live long and prosper; the righteous suffer hardships, etc.

Who understands the logic of divine providence? How does one live happily with unsearchable and unpredictable providence? The answer is right here. This chapter prepares Christians to live with divine providence as follows:

1. Relax in God's hand – *Ecclesiastes 9:1-6*.
2. Reap spiritual rewards and have fun along the way – *Ecclesiastes 9:7-10*.
3. Rest in God's will – *Ecclesiastes 9:11-12*.
4. Rule life with wisdom – *Ecclesiastes 9:13-18*.

Ecclesiastes 9:1 For all this I considered in my heart even to declare all this, that the righteous, and the wise, and their works, are in the hand of God: no man knoweth either love or hatred by all that is before them. (2) All things come alike to all: there is one event to the righteous, and to the wicked; to the good and to the clean, and to the unclean; to him that sacrificeth, and to him that sacrificeth not: as is the good, so is the sinner; and he that sweareth, as he that feareth an oath. (3) This is an evil among all things that are done under the sun, that there is one event unto all: yea, also the heart of the sons of men is full of evil, and madness is in their heart while they live, and after that they go to the dead.

The work of providence is indiscriminate in that the righteous and the wicked are subject to the same life circumstances. Bad things can happen to good people, and good things can happen to bad people. (This just destroyed karma.) And no one knows what the future brings. The difference, however, is that the righteous and their works rest in God's hand, while the wicked go to the dead.

There are many uncertainties in this world, but we can count on these five things, according to the above three verses:

1. The righteous and the wicked fare alike in this world.
   Beginning with verse 2, it is common to think and expect the righteous to have a better life than the wicked. However, in reality, the righteous and the wicked are subject to the same vanity. *Ecclesiastes 8:14a There is a vanity which is done upon the earth; that there be just men, unto whom it happeneth according to the work of the wicked; again, there be wicked men, to whom it happeneth according to the work of the righteous.* The piety of the righteous cannot counteract the work of providence. After all, do not wheat (the righteous) and tares (the wicked or ungodly) grow in the same field under the same elements and share the same resources? Whatever happens to the wheat happens also to the tares, and vice-versa—*"all things come alike to all."*

2. Death happens to all.
   The wheat and the tares share a common fate; both are killed at harvest—*"there is one event to the righteous, and to the wicked."* The body of the righteous and the ungodly will die and reduce to dust, because both have

sinned, and *"the wages of sin is death."* Death is bad. Here, it is said to be *"an evil among all things that are done under the sun."*

3. The ungodly will live foolishly.
    From the ungodly standpoint, the righteous have no advantage over the wicked, because they are not immune from sufferings. What's the point of serving God who allows bad things to happen to good people? Why join a church, which is an organized religion with ecclesiastical machinery that conforms people and takes their money? Why submit to the Bible as the final authority? Why not live like hell, which is natural? Instead of repenting of their sins, the ungodly double down on folly—*"the heart of the sons of men is full of evil, and madness is in their heart while they live."* They have a heart issue that drives them to live foolishly and make bad choices. *Jeremiah 17:9 The heart is deceitful above all things, and desperately wicked: who can know it?* (This destroys the ideology that humans are inherently good. *Psalms 14:3 They are all gone aside, they are all together become filthy: there is none that doeth good, no, not one.*) Those who trust their hearts instead of God and His truth are fools. *Proverbs 28:26 He that trusteth in his own heart is a fool: but whoso walketh wisely, he shall be delivered.*

4. All who die in sin go to the dead.
    No matter how the ungodly live their lives, they will eventually die, or more precisely *"go to the dead,"* to join those without hope of eternal life in hell. *1John 5:12 He that hath the Son hath life; and he that hath not the Son of God hath not life.* All who reject Jesus Christ as Lord and Savior will die in their sins. *John 8:24 I said therefore unto you, that ye shall die in your sins: for if ye*

believe not that I am he, ye shall die in your sins. Did you know that a person can be in hell for 1,000 years and it is only day one? Pause to think about it.

5. God cares for the righteous.
    Though the righteous and the ungodly fare much alike in this world, the righteous have a clear advantage in that their lives and works are in God's hand. That's a great place to be. Consider Jesus' words in *John 10:27-30, "My sheep hear my voice, and I know them, and they follow me: And I give unto them eternal life; and they shall never perish, neither shall any man pluck them out of my hand. My Father, which gave them me, is greater than all; and no man is able to pluck them out of my Father's hand. I and my Father are one."* The righteous need not despair when things are not in their favor or when it seems God deals harshly with them. *1Peter 4:12 Beloved, think it not strange concerning the fiery trial which is to try you, as though some strange thing happened unto you: (13) But rejoice, inasmuch as ye are partakers of Christ's sufferings; that, when his glory shall be revealed, ye may be glad also with exceeding joy.* The righteous can rest in God's eternal security and continue to serve Him. They know that their external circumstances do not reflect God's feelings toward them.

    The righteous, however, must be conscientious of their works, because God will grade them. *1Corinthians 3:13 Every man's work shall be made manifest: for the day shall declare it, because it shall be revealed by fire; and the fire shall try every man's work of what sort it is. (14) If any man's work abide which he hath built thereupon, he shall receive a reward. (15) If any man's work shall be burned, he shall suffer loss: but he himself shall be saved; yet so as by fire.*

Ecclesiastes 9:4 For to him that is joined to all the living there is hope: for a living dog is better than a dead lion. (5) For the living know that they shall die: but the dead know not any thing, neither have they any more a reward; for the memory of them is forgotten. (6) Also their love, and their hatred, and their envy, is now perished; neither have they any more a portion for ever in any thing that is done under the sun.

Continuing with the thought from verse 3, it doesn't pay to live sinfully and go to the dead. What good is a hopeless dead person?

Isn't a living dog better than a hopeless dead lion? Put differently, isn't the meanest person alive better than the noblest person who is dead without hope? What's the point of being the king of the beasts if life is limited to this world with no hope in the afterlife? People who aspire to be the greatest in this world but are without hope of eternal life, be forewarned. You will die someday, and when that day comes, you are worse than a "living dog". In death, everything perishes:

- End of the hearing of the blessed word of reconciliation. The ungodly who are alive are better off than the dead. Even though they too will kick the bucket someday, for now they are under God's grace and have access to His saving knowledge. Read *Psalms 19:1-6, Proverbs 1:20-23*. There is hope for them to repent of sins. However, it is game over for the ungodly who are numbered with the dead. By living an ungodly life driven by a heart that is full of evil and trusting in uncertain riches, they squander their portion under the sun, which is their only opportunity to repent and be right with God. In death,

they will no longer hear the saving knowledge of God—
"the dead know not any thing."

- End of all enjoyments.
  "Neither have they any more a reward" – The ungodly
  do not have spiritual fruits. The earthly fruits of their
  labor do not go with them, but rather are enjoyed by
  others.

- End of memories.
  "The memory of them is forgotten" – The memories that
  the ungodly worked so hard to perpetuate will soon be
  forgotten. *Proverbs 10:7 The memory of the just is
  blessed: but the name of the wicked shall rot.*

- End of affections and enmities.
  *"Also their love, and their hatred, and their envy, is now
  perished"* – What can a dead person do to or for others?
  (What's the point in praying to or through the dead?
  What can Mother Mary and Buddha do for anyone?
  They are still in their graves. Hey, Jesus Christ is risen; He
  is alive! He is the only mediator between God and man.
  *1Timothy 2:5 For there is one God, and one mediator
  between God and men, the man Christ Jesus.*)

In death, it is too late to repent of sins. Read about the rich
man who died and went to hell in *Luke 16:19-31*. Now is the time to
repent and be right with God by accepting Jesus Christ as Lord.
*Romans 10:9 That if thou shalt confess with thy mouth the Lord
Jesus, and shalt believe in thine heart that God hath raised him from
the dead, thou shalt be saved. (10) For with the heart man believeth
unto righteousness; and with the mouth confession is made unto
salvation.* Read *John 3:1-21*.

Christians, take comfort. The Bible says we are more than conquerors. We can relax in God's hands— *"the righteous, and the wise, and their works, are in the hand of God."*

Ecclesiastes 9:7 Go thy way, eat thy bread with joy, and drink thy wine with a merry heart; for God now accepteth thy works. (8) Let thy garments be always white; and let thy head lack no ointment. (9) Live joyfully with the wife whom thou lovest all the days of the life of thy vanity, which he hath given thee under the sun, all the days of thy vanity: for that is thy portion in this life, and in thy labour which thou takest under the sun. (10) Whatsoever thy hand findeth to do, do it with thy might; for there is no work, nor device, nor knowledge, nor wisdom, in the grave, whither thou goest.

Seeing that death is certain and the day of death is unknown, the righteous should diligently serve God, reap spiritual fruits, and have fun along the way. Following is how the righteous should live their lives in this temporal world:

- Mind the way.
  "Go thy way..." – The righteous are free to enjoy life, because God accepts their ministry and service. The righteous should comfortably and cheerfully enjoy the fruit of their labor. Use everything in moderation, keeping in mind *1Corinthians 10:23, "All things are lawful for me, but all things are not expedient: all things are lawful for me, but all things edify not."*

- Mind the testimony.
  "Let thy garments be always white" – The righteous should keep their testimony by living a blameless life. (Blameless does not mean sinless.) *Philippians 2:15 That ye may be blameless and harmless, the sons of God,*

without rebuke, in the midst of a crooked and perverse nation, among whom ye shine as lights in the world.

- Mind the unity of the brethren.
  "Let thy head lack no ointment" – The righteous should keep the fellowship and unity of the brethren. These are our fellow soldiers. It is good to have buddies in foxholes. *Psalms 133:1 Behold, how good and how pleasant it is for brethren to dwell together in unity! (2) It is like the precious ointment upon the head, that ran down upon the beard, even Aaron's beard: that went down to the skirts of his garments; (3) As the dew of Hermon, and as the dew that descended upon the mountains of Zion: for there the LORD commanded the blessing, even life for evermore.*

- Mind the indispensable ministry partner.
  "Live joyfully with the wife whom thou lovest all the days of the life of thy vanity..." – As God gave Eve to Adam to accomplish his work, God will give every minister a wife for the same purpose. (Every believer is a minister.) The wife is a help meet, according to *Genesis 2:18-24.* A help meet is first and foremost an indispensable ministry partner. Without this proper understanding, a marriage is usually built on the desires of the flesh.

  Husbands should love their wives, live joyfully with them, rejoice in their embrace, and keep in mind that the purpose of the matrimony hasn't changed since the first marriage. *Ephesians 5:25 Husbands, love your wives, even as Christ also loved the church, and gave himself for it.* Read *Proverbs 5.*

- Mind the kingdom business.

"Whatsoever thy hand findeth to do, do it with thy might..." – Be diligent about the Father's business, because we know not the day of death (*Genesis 27:2*).

Realize that the Holy Spirit of God distributes spiritual gifts to every believer to profit the body of Christ (the church) holistically. Read *1Corinthians 12:4-11.* Not sure what your spiritual gifts are? The way to find out is to be diligent in the work of ministry and service, and God will show you where you belong.

Ecclesiastes 9:11 I returned, and saw under the sun, that the race is not to the swift, nor the battle to the strong, neither yet bread to the wise, nor yet riches to men of understanding, nor yet favour to men of skill; but time and chance happeneth to them all. (12) For man also knoweth not his time: as the fishes that are taken in an evil net, and as the birds that are caught in the snare; so are the sons of men snared in an evil time, when it falleth suddenly upon them.

Having urged people to be diligent in verse 10, Solomon now cautions people not to trust in their own strength or wisdom, but rather to submit to God's will for the outcome of things. This is due to a phenomenon under the sun—*"the race is not to the swift, nor the battle to the strong, neither yet bread to the wise, nor yet riches to men of understanding, nor yet favour to men of skill."* Like piety, strength and wisdom also cannot counteract the work of providence.

We do the work the best we can, but we should not count on our skills or intellectual prowess for success and happiness. If we succeed, give God the glory; if we do not succeed, humbly submit to His will. This goes back to *Ecclesiastes 9:1b, "The righteous, and the wise, and their works, are in the hand of God: no man knoweth either love or hatred by all that is before them."*

The work of providence is so arbitrary and unpredictable that people who cannot resolve it simply attribute it to *"time and chance"* or opportunistic luck. In a sense, good things happen to certain people because of their dumb luck, and bad things happen to some because they are at the wrong place at the wrong time. The reality is that nothing is left to chance, but God is in control of everything, including the time of death, which only He knows.

Let not the fastest, strongest, wisest, richest, and most skillful people be cocky, because they are just like fish and birds at the time of death. Death ensnares people as it ensnares fish and birds, and no one knows when it will be.

What's the righteous to do in this case? We must not delay in serving God, because we know not when the opportunity will end.

Ecclesiastes 9:13 This wisdom have I seen also under the sun, and it seemed great unto me: (14) There was a little city, and few men within it; and there came a great king against it, and besieged it, and built great bulwarks against it: (15) Now there was found in it a poor wise man, and he by his wisdom delivered the city; yet no man remembered that same poor man. (16) Then said I, Wisdom is better than strength: nevertheless the poor man's wisdom is despised, and his words are not heard. (17) The words of wise men are heard in quiet more than the cry of him that ruleth among fools. (18) Wisdom is better than weapons of war: but one sinner destroyeth much good.

Even though wisdom is not able to counteract the work of providence, it is still incredibly useful to individuals, regardless of social status. Featured in the above verses is a story of a poor wise man, who by his wisdom saved the lives of all his fellows.

There is a particular wisdom available under the sun that seems great to Solomon—the wisdom that delivers people from death and destruction of war.

An important truth is hidden behind the simple story of a poor wise man who delivered his city from a great king. Have you ever wondered why a great king goes through such great lengths in besieging a small city with few people in it? Why doesn't he just crush it with his mighty army?

The great king is the devil and the small city is us. The devil wages a spiritual war against us and would destroy us if not for the wisdom of God, personified by Jesus Christ, who made Himself poor and of no reputation. *1Corinthians 1:24 But unto them which are called, both Jews and Greeks, Christ the power of God, and the wisdom of God. Philippians 2:6 Who, being in the form of God, thought it not robbery to be equal with God: (7) But made himself of no reputation, and took upon him the form of a servant, and was made in the likeness of men: (8) And being found in fashion as a man, he humbled himself, and became obedient unto death, even the death of the cross.*

Because of the wisdom of God, the devil has to build a great bulwark to protect himself against us, the little guys. Jesus Christ is the great Wisdom that delivers us from death and destruction by our principal enemy. But we shouldn't hold our breath waiting for the world to congratulate us, because it despises Jesus Christ. *Isaiah 53:3 He is despised and rejected of men; a man of sorrows, and acquainted with grief: and we hid as it were our faces from him; he was despised, and we esteemed him not.*

We must recognize that we are surrounded by our spiritual enemy. If the devil cannot take us into hell fire, he will take the fire of serving God out of us. The wisdom of God is our protection.

Wisdom is better than strength, because we cannot rely on the flesh to fight a spiritual battle. *1Timothy 4:8 For bodily exercise profiteth little: but godliness is profitable unto all things, having promise of the life that now is, and of that which is to come.* *Ecclesiastes 9:11b* says, *"The race is not to the swift, nor the battle to the strong."* We must be equipped with and live the word of God to overcome our spiritual battles.

The world, however, despises the reconciliatory words of wisdom and looks to its hero, who is a blustering fool ruling among fools. *Proverbs 1:20 Wisdom crieth without; she uttereth her voice in the streets: (21) She crieth in the chief place of concourse, in the openings of the gates: in the city she uttereth her words, saying, (22) How long, ye simple ones, will ye love simplicity? and the scorners delight in their scorning, and fools hate knowledge? (23) Turn you at my reproof: behold, I will pour out my spirit unto you, I will make known my words unto you. (24) Because I have called, and ye refused; I have stretched out my hand, and no man regarded; (25) But ye have set at nought all my counsel, and would none of my reproof.*

Wisdom is also better than weapons of war. *Isaiah 54:17 No weapon that is formed against thee shall prosper; and every tongue that shall rise against thee in judgment thou shalt condemn. This is the heritage of the servants of the LORD, and their righteousness is of me, saith the LORD.* But the righteous must beware of sin, as it can destroy much good. We cannot have it both ways. We cannot expect God's protection and blessings and live like the world.

Final Thoughts

In life, we will experience circumstances and events that are bad, hurtful, unexplainable, and illogical. Instead of being mad at God, we should resign to accept the things that are beyond our control and remember *Romans 8:28, "And we know that all things work together for good to them that love God, to them who are the called according to his purpose."* The Bible also states, *"For I reckon that the sufferings of this present time are not worthy to be compared with the glory which shall be revealed in us."* (*Romans 8:18*)

The wisdom for living with providence and persevering in our service to God is found in this chapter. In this world, the righteous and the wicked fare alike, but it will not be the same in the world to come. This world is not our home. We remain here for the time being to replicate the works of our Lord. *John 14:12 Verily, verily, I say unto you, He that believeth on me, the works that I do shall he do also; and greater works than these shall he do; because I go unto my Father.*

We can rest assured that, *"the righteous, and the wise, and their works, are in the hand of God."* May God grant you grace and peace and accept your work of faith.

15 – Living with Bad Civil Government

"Our leadership is stupid; these are stupid people. We are led by very, very stupid people." – Donald Trump on the U.S. government during the presidential campaign.

"Government is not the solution to our problem. Government is the problem." – President Ronald Reagan

Besides the ability to live with divine providence, Christians must also be able to operate and live with bad civil governments. Featured herein are the counsels of wisdom that help the righteous cope with bad governments.

1. Guard against the folly of fools – *Ecclesiastes 10:1-3*
2. Guard against the folly of uprising – *Ecclesiastes 10:4-11*
3. Guard against the folly of words – *Ecclesiastes 10:12-15*
4. Guard against irreverent words and thoughts – *Ecclesiastes 10:16-20*

Ecclesiastes 10:1 Dead flies cause the ointment of the apothecary to send forth a stinking savour: so doth a little folly him that is in reputation for wisdom and honour. (2) A wise man's heart is at his right hand; but a fool's heart at his left. (3) Yea also, when he that is a fool walketh by the way, his wisdom faileth him, and he saith to every one that he is a fool.

To successfully live and operate under the rule of a bad civil government, Christians must choose God's wisdom over the wisdom of the world. The above three verses instruct the wise to guard against the folly of fools, the foolish mind, and the foolish way.

In the same way that it only takes a tiny dead fly to stink up the sweet perfume of the apothecary, it only takes a little folly to ruin a person's good reputation of wisdom and honor established over time with a great deal of effort. Folly is like leaven. *Galatians 5:9 A little leaven leaveneth the whole lump.*

The folly of fools is rooted in worldly wisdom. The wisdom of the world says the Bible is antiquated and that something more modern and culturally relevant is needed. Mix in a few worldly concepts. Listen to Dr. so and so with millions of followers. See the proofs here and there. Don't worry, you will still look holy and godly.

All it takes is a little bit of the world's philosophy—a little bit of sin to ruin our walk with the Lord. *Colossians 2:8 Beware lest any man spoil you through philosophy and vain deceit, after the tradition of men, after the rudiments of the world, and not after Christ.*

Many faithful believers, including pastors and church leaders, drop like flies because they make affinity with the world. Solomon made affinity with Pharaoh, king of Egypt, according to *1Kings 3:1.* (Egypt is a type of the world.) How did life work out for Solomon? Read *1Kings 11.* Jehoshaphat, the king of Judah, made affinity with Ahab (a type of antichrist), according to *2Chronicles 18:1.* Consequently, the wrath of God was upon Jehoshaphat. Read *2Chronicles 18, 2Chronicles 19:2.*

Sadly, churches are sucking up worldly philosophies for ministry like giant street vacuum machines.

We need to know the word of God to fend against worldly wisdom. What wisdom do you rely on for happiness and for raising children? Your wisdom will help or fail you depending on the placement of your heart—at the right or the left.

The heart or mind of the wise is said to be at the right hand. In the Bible, the right hand is the hand of salvation (*Psalms 18:35, Psalms 20:6*), righteousness (*Deuteronomy 33:2, Mark 16:19, 1Peter 3:22*), power (*Exodus 15:6*), and blessing (*Genesis 48:8-22*). In other words, the heart of the wise desires the things above and not of the world.

For most people, the right hand is the useful and helpful hand. *Psalms 16:8 I have set the LORD always before me: because he is at my right hand, I shall not be moved.* Is the word of God at your right hand?

The heart or mind of fools is said to be at the left hand and is worldly. Their mind and affections are set on the things of the world and not on things of God.

And then there is the foolish way. As a result of choosing the world's wisdom over God's words, fools are at a loss and constantly make bad choices. Their way of life is guided by their sinful heart that is tuned to the world instead of the Bible. They would have none of God's counsels and reproofs. *Proverbs 19:3 The foolishness of man perverteth his way: and his heart fretteth against the LORD.* What initially seems good and makes sense ends up being a disaster. *Proverbs 14:12 There is a way which seemeth right unto a man, but the end thereof are the ways of death.* The wisdom of fools is to build the house (life) upon the sand (shifting and uncertain wisdom), but God's wisdom is to build the house upon a rock (Jesus Christ). Read *Matthew 7:24-27*. Their wisdom will fail them and their folly will become obvious. They will finally confess, "I am such an idiot!"

Ecclesiastes 10:4 If the spirit of the ruler rise up against thee, leave not thy place; for yielding pacifieth great offences. (5) There is an evil which I have seen under the sun, as an error which proceedeth from the ruler: (6) Folly is set in great dignity, and the rich sit in low place. (7) I have seen servants upon horses, and princes walking as servants upon the earth.

Here is a powder keg situation ready to explode. Idiots are in charge, while capable and talented people (referred to as the rich in verse 6,) are demoted to sit in low places. Idiots make stupid policies that impact your livelihood.

How frequently this happens in the workplace! A clueless person gets promoted to the director or vice president level and makes crazy changes that impact your future at the company. How upset will you be? How far will you go to correct the situation? Will you be outraged and conduct yourself insolently toward your management?

This also happens in governments, where the foolish cronies of the rulers get preferential treatment. People who are unfit to rule go on horseback (a mark of distinction), while people with real experience go on foot and are despised. The promotion of Haman is a good example. *Esther 3:1 After these things did king Ahasuerus promote Haman the son of Hammedatha the Agagite, and advanced him, and set his seat above all the princes that were with him. (2) And all the king's servants, that were in the king's gate, bowed, and reverenced Haman: for the king had so commanded concerning him. But Mordecai bowed not, nor did him reverence.*

Get used to it. It is an evil that happens only under the sun, but not in heaven. God does not make this mistake. It is a human error of the ruling class, both in the private and public sectors.

You may give your piece-of-mind good advice at an open forum with management, or colorfully write about the real improvements that should be made in an "anonymous" employee survey. The management may not appreciate your counsel and may come after you. If you find yourself in this situation, the solution is to calmly yield to the ruler's anger. Humble yourself and remember what the Bible says about pacifying anger. *Proverbs 15:1 A soft answer turneth away wrath: but grievous words stir up anger. Proverbs 25:15 By long forbearing is a prince persuaded, and a soft tongue breaketh the bone.* Do not escalate the situation and quit your job to rebel. (While it is the ruler's error to promote fools, it is your error to rebel.) *Ecclesiastes 8:3 Be not hasty to go out of his sight: stand not in an evil thing; for he doeth whatsoever pleaseth him.* It is far safer to yield than to contend with the ruler.

The wisdom of God instructs you to guard against the folly of uprising. The following verses warn against mischievous and malicious deeds that will backfire and hurt you.

Ecclesiastes 10:8 He that diggeth a pit shall fall into it; and whoso breaketh an hedge, a serpent shall bite him. (9) Whoso removeth stones shall be hurt therewith; and he that cleaveth wood shall be endangered thereby.

Remember the good old cartoon characters Wile E. Coyote and Tom the cat? Their numerous ingenious attempts to capture and eat the Road Runner and Jerry the mouse always backfired with mayhem and destruction that hurt them instead. People typically try to overturn a ruler or governor they don't like with the following attacks, but the above verses warn against treason.

- An attempt against the ruler's life – "*He that diggeth a pit shall fall into it.*" The trap you set might catch you. Treason is dangerous, because you might get the life sentence. *Proverbs 26:27 Whoso diggeth a pit shall fall therein: and he that rolleth a stone, it will return upon him. Psalms 7:15 He made a pit, and digged it, and is fallen into the ditch which he made. (16) His mischief shall return upon his own head, and his violent dealing shall come down upon his own pate.* Read *Psalms 35:7, Psalms 57:6.*

- An attempt against the ruler's security – *"Whoso breaketh an hedge, a serpent shall bite him."* In the Bible, a hedge is a form of protection and security. You need to know what is inside the hedge before breaking it down, otherwise, you risk the deadly poison of the ruler. Read *Proverbs 3:29.*

- An attempt against the ruler's governing structure – *"Whoso removeth stones shall be hurt therewith."* It is not easy to subvert the settled structure of a bad government in order to redress your particular grievances. It will be like pulling down a settled stone wall. Chances are, you will get hurt by the falling pieces and increase your suffering.

- An attempt to split the government – *"He that cleaveth wood shall be endangered thereby."* Similar to removing stones, it is also dangerous to split an established government, especially if you have such sorry tools as in verse 10a below—*"If the iron be blunt, and he do not whet the edge, then must he put to more strength."*

Ecclesiastes 10:10 If the iron be blunt, and he do not whet the edge, then must he put to more strength: but wisdom is profitable to direct. (11) Surely the serpent will bite without enchantment; and a babbler is no better.

Would you battle a bad ruler with a blunt weapon? You might if you are not directed by the wisdom of God that is sharper than any two-edged sword. *Ecclesiastes 9:18a Wisdom is better than weapons of war.*

If you don't know how to apply God's words to life's problems, you will go through life the hard way. It would be like splitting wood with a dull axe, exerting a lot of effort without much progress, increasing your suffering instead. *Ecclesiastes 9:16a Then said I, Wisdom is better than strength.*

So as not to increase your present suffering under a bad ruler, you need to *"whet the edge"* or sharpen your knowledge of God's words and let wisdom direct you to the proper course of action.

For example, if a ruler is coming after you like a provoked serpent that is ready to bite, it is futile to babble your way out of the snake bite. You must exercise the art of charming based on God's words. The pure wisdom of God will never lead you to rebel against authority or to go to battle with a blunt iron. It teaches the way of peace and is gentle, enabling you to enchant the ruler with your humble submission. *James 3:13 Who is a wise man and endued with knowledge among you? let him shew out of a good conversation his works with meekness of wisdom. (14) But if ye have bitter envying and strife in your hearts, glory not, and lie not against the truth. (15) This wisdom descendeth not from above, but is earthly, sensual, devilish. (16) For where envying and strife is, there is confusion and every evil work. (17) But the wisdom that is from above is first pure, then peaceable, gentle, and easy to be intreated, full of mercy and good fruits, without partiality, and without hypocrisy. (18) And the fruit of righteousness is sown in peace of them that make peace.*

Ecclesiastes 10:12 The words of a wise man's mouth are gracious; but the lips of a fool will swallow up himself. (13) The beginning of the words of his mouth is foolishness: and the end of his talk is mischievous madness. (14) A fool also is full of words: a man cannot tell what shall be; and what shall be after him, who can tell him? (15) The labour of the foolish wearieth every one of them, because he knoweth not how to go to the city.

The wisdom of God also instructs you to guard against the folly of words. Your words may dignify or destroy you. Think before you speak. Consider this acronym:

> T – Is it true?
> H – Is it helpful?
> I – Is it inspiring?
> N – Is it necessary?
> K – Is it kind?

If what you are about to say is not gracious, bite your tongue. *Ephesians 4:29 Let no corrupt communication proceed out of your mouth, but that which is good to the use of edifying, that it may minister grace unto the hearers.* King David prayed to God, "*Set a watch, O LORD, before my mouth; keep the door of my lips.*" (*Psalms 141:3*)

The courteous, polite, and gracious words of the wise win friends and gain them favor. *Proverbs 22:11 He that loveth pureness of heart, for the grace of his lips the king shall be his friend.* If the wise find themselves in the situation in *Ecclesiastes 10:4*, they know to use conciliatory language to charm the angry ruler and get out of trouble. But the words of fools destroy them. *Proverbs 18:6 A fool's lips enter into contention, and his mouth calleth for strokes. Proverbs 18:7 A fool's mouth is his destruction, and his lips are the snare of his soul. Proverbs 12:13 The wicked is snared by the transgression of his lips: but the just shall come out of trouble. Proverbs 12:18 There is that speaketh like the piercings of a sword: but the tongue of the wise is health.*

Following are the three characteristics of fools:

- Fools talk nonsense – *"The beginning of the words of his mouth is foolishness: and the end of his talk is mischievous madness."* They start out talking nonsense out of the abundance of folly in their hearts. As they go on, the nonsense becomes more intense. Absurdity pours out of their mouths. *Proverbs 15:2 The tongue of the wise useth knowledge aright: but the mouth of fools poureth out foolishness.* The end of all their yack is mischievous madness and insanity that does nobody good.

- Fools talk a lot – *"A fool also is full of words."* Fools are know-it-alls who love to chat about profound and mysterious subjects, like future events. They prate and drown their listeners in a multitude of words in order to show they are knowledgeable and right. No one knows what the future holds, except prating fools who think they are so smart. They would be smart to shut up, but they can't. *Proverbs 17:28 Even a fool, when he holdeth his peace, is counted wise: and he that shutteth his lips is esteemed a man of understanding.*

- Fools are lost – *"He knoweth not how to go to the city."* The labor of fools is wearisome, because they work hard to prove and justify their absurdity. They are so ignorant that they miss the obvious and well-known path to a city.

  Fools miss the city of God, because they begin their speeches with the nonsense, "There is no God." *Psalms 14:1a The fool hath said in his heart, There is no God.* Then they give their listeners an earful on how things began with a big bang and evolved from there. And they labor tirelessly to prove they are right. *Proverbs 12:15*

The way of a fool is right in his own eyes: but he that hearkeneth unto counsel is wise.

The Bible has two seemingly contradicting methods for handling fools, but a closer read shows that one is for our protection and the other is for their protection. *Proverbs 26:4 Answer not a fool according to his folly, <u>lest thou</u> also be like unto him. Proverbs 26:5 Answer a fool according to his folly, <u>lest he</u> be wise in his own conceit.* We are to know when to keep silent and when to speak. On one hand, we don't want to debate and argue with fools, because we risk being like them. When they boast themselves in nonsense, we are not to top that with nonsense, as in fighting fire with fire. The reason we answer fools is for their own good—to keep them from further damaging themselves in their folly. We do this in wisdom. However, if they will not hear the words of wisdom, just leave them alone. *Proverbs 14:7 Go from the presence of a foolish man, when thou perceivest not in him the lips of knowledge.*

Ecclesiastes 10:16 Woe to thee, O land, when thy king is a child, and thy princes eat in the morning! (17) Blessed art thou, O land, when thy king is the son of nobles, and thy princes eat in due season, for strength, and not for drunkenness!

Here is another explosive reality of bad government—rulers give themselves to pleasures instead of governing.

Excessive sensual pleasures have a way of ruining individuals and entire societies. (Review the trial that Solomon made on mirth in Chapter 5.) When rulers indulge in pleasures, they become childish and neglect their duties. They should be dispensing justice in the morning (*Jeremiah 21:12*), but instead, they are busy fulfilling their lusts, making themselves unfit for service. (We are now seeing waves of sexual misconduct allegations crashing against the U.S. Capitol, toppling powerful lawmakers and bringing an abrupt end to their careers.) *Isaiah 5:11 Woe unto them that rise up early in the morning, that they may follow strong drink; that continue until night, till wine inflame them!* Their foolishness brings great sorrow and distress to the nation. "Government is like a baby. An alimentary canal with a big appetite at one end and no sense of responsibility at the other." – President Ronald Reagan.

In contrast, happy is the nation that is governed by nobles (not just aristocratic in blood or political or social status, but wise rulers who execute justice, and judgment, and equity, according to the instructions of wisdom.) These rulers do not run after the pleasures of this world. They *"eat in due season"* (in proper time) for strength in order to perform their duties and not for feasting or revelry.

Ecclesiastes 10:18 By much slothfulness the building decayeth; and through idleness of the hands the house droppeth through.

It takes a lot of effort to maintain a government and keep its people safe, healthy, and happy. Many rulers elected to public office quickly forget their charters and mandates and bask in their passion and power, pleasuring themselves in their ivory tower. Only a handful would work hard for the people who elected them.

Rulers given to folly and pleasures will be the ruin of a nation. Their reckless habits lead to slothfulness at first, followed by complete negligence of duties. The nation becomes disorganized, begins to decay, and degrades to ruin. As a house with decayed rafters and beams, if not fixed, the roof will cave in.

Likewise for individuals, much effort is required to maintain both the physical and spiritual life. We need physical food for physical strength and spiritual food for spiritual strength. We must maintain our physical bodies, which are God's temples, for His service through healthy living. We must also keep our spirit fed with prayer, the word of God, and the fellowship of believers. However, if we indulge in the pleasures of folly, we will slack and eventually neglect the maintenance, which will be to our ruin.

If we have time for folly, something is decaying in our lives. But if we properly maintain our physical and spiritual lives, we will not have time for folly.

Ecclesiastes 10:19 A feast is made for laughter, and wine maketh merry: but money answereth all things. (20) Curse not the king, no not in thy thought; and curse not the rich in thy bedchamber: for a bird of the air shall carry the voice, and that which hath wings shall tell the matter.

The pleasures of folly are not cheap to maintain. Rulers who indulge in pleasures must find a way to fund them, usually in the form of higher taxes, because more money is the answer to their sin. Doing so adds sorrow to the people they serve.

Even so, do not revile the rulers or their officers—not in words or in thoughts, nor in public or in the bedchamber (the most secret place). Do not speak irreverently or contemptuously of them. This is because words have a mysterious way of getting out, as if a bird hears your saying and repeats it. This is similar to the idiom, "Hedges have eyes, and walls have ears." How many times have we seen a private conversation being secretly recorded, making news, and getting the speaker in trouble? Believers and missionaries operating in countries with no freedom of speech and hostile to Christianity take heed. People lose their lives over what they say, and no mercy can be expected from such an administration.

What's the point of cursing the rulers when our curse has no power? On the flip side, if they hear of our contemptuous words, they may curse us in return, and their words carry power. The Bible instructs us to pray for them and to do good works. *1Timothy 2:1 I exhort therefore, that, first of all, supplications, prayers, intercessions, and giving of thanks, be made for all men; (2) For kings, and for all that are in authority; that we may lead a quiet and peaceable life in all godliness and honesty. Romans 13:3 For rulers are not a terror to good works, but to the evil. Wilt thou then not be afraid of the power? do that which is good, and thou shalt have praise of the same: (4) For he is the minister of God to thee for good. But if thou do that which is evil, be afraid; for he beareth not the sword in vain: for he is the minister of God, a revenger to execute wrath upon him that doeth evil.*

Final Thoughts

There is no good human government on earth. The human nature is corrupt, and many are without a moral compass. Many rulers abuse power to serve and profit self. *Matthew 20:25 But Jesus called them unto him, and said, Ye know that the princes of the Gentiles exercise dominion over them, and they that are great exercise authority upon them. (26) But it shall not be so among you: but whosoever will be great among you, let him be your minister; (27) And whosoever will be chief among you, let him be your servant: (28) Even as the Son of man came not to be ministered unto, but to minister, and to give his life a ransom for many.*

As God's servants, we are to operate wisely in taking the gospel to all parts of the world. This includes countries run by religious authoritarian regimes that are hostile to Christianity. *Matthew 28:19 Go ye therefore, and teach all nations, baptizing them in the name of the Father, and of the Son, and of the Holy Ghost: (20) Teaching them to observe all things whatsoever I have commanded you: and, lo, I am with you alway, even unto the end of the world. Amen. Matthew 10:16 Behold, I send you forth as sheep in the midst of wolves: be ye therefore wise as serpents, and harmless as doves.*

Even in such relatively safe countries as the U.S., Canada, and Great Britain, it is better to pray for authorities than to spray mean words at them. We ought not to pray because we desire a good life, but that we may be able to exercise our faith and minister the gospel in relative peace and safety. May God give you the wisdom to survive, thrive, and bear spiritual fruit in every country.

16 – Live Out Your Calling

magine hearing these words when you stand before the Lord, *"Well done, thou good and faithful servant: thou hast been faithful over a few things, I will make thee ruler over many things: enter thou into the joy of thy lord."* Immediately, you are ecstatic as all your service to the Lord pays off. You forget the hardship of ministry.

Now imagine hearing these words, *"Thou wicked and slothful servant,"* as you lock eyes with the Lord who died for your sins. Regret, shame, and sadness enshroud you as you weep bitterly, like Peter when he denied knowing the Lord three times.

The key to hearing the praise of God is to live out our calling. This life is a 70-year boot camp that prepares us to meet our Savior at the Judgment Seat of Christ. Let us not faint in the work of ministry, and let us bring in the sheaves to meet Him.

Featured herein is the call to fulfill the Great Commission:

- Fulfill our duty to God before His judgment falls upon sinners – Ecclesiastes 11:1-6
- Fulfill our duty to God before the infirmities of old age fall upon us – Ecclesiastes 11:7–12:7

Ecclesiastes 11:1 Cast thy bread upon the waters: for thou shalt find it after many days. (2) Give a portion to seven, and also to eight; for thou knowest not what evil shall be upon the earth. (3) If the clouds be full of rain, they empty themselves upon the earth:

and if the tree fall toward the south, or toward the north, in the place where the tree falleth, there it shall be.

Many preachers and teachers use this passage of scripture to encourage people to be charitable. While that is a good thing, a significant message of far greater importance is hidden in this passage. The following keys help to decode the message:

- Bread represents the word of God. Jesus Christ was the personification of the bread of life who came down from heaven. *John 6:35 And Jesus said unto them, I am the bread of life: he that cometh to me shall never hunger; and he that believeth on me shall never thirst.*

- Waters represent the masses of people. *Revelation 17:15 And he saith unto me, The waters which thou sawest, where the whore sitteth, are peoples, and multitudes, and nations, and tongues.*

- The number seven is the number of perfection or completeness. It also marks the end of a thing. *Genesis 2:2 And on the seventh day God ended his work which he had made; and he rested on the seventh day from all his work which he had made.*

- Following the completion represented by the number seven, the number eight signifies a new beginning. After God wiped humanity off the earth with Noah's flood, He repopulated the earth with eight people. *1Peter 3:18 For Christ also hath once suffered for sins, the just for the unjust, that he might bring us to God, being put to death in the flesh, but quickened by the Spirit: (19) By which also he went and preached unto the spirits in prison; (20) Which sometime were disobedient, when once the longsuffering of God waited in the days of Noah, while the ark was a preparing, wherein few, that is, eight souls were saved by water.*

- In the Bible, clouds are connected with the second coming of the Lord Jesus Christ. *Mark 14:62 And Jesus said, I am: and ye shall see the Son of man sitting on the right hand of power, and coming in the clouds of heaven. Revelation 1:7 Behold, he cometh with clouds; and every eye shall see him, and they also which pierced him: and all kindreds of the earth shall wail because of him. Even so, Amen.*

- Trees typify people. *Psalm 1:1 Blessed is the man that walketh not in the counsel of the ungodly, nor standeth in the way of sinners, nor sitteth in the seat of the scornful. (2) But his delight is in the law of the LORD; and in his law doth he meditate day and night. (3) And he shall be like a tree planted by the rivers of water, that bringeth forth his fruit in his season; his leaf also shall not wither; and whatsoever he doeth shall prosper.*

With these keys and their respective representations, what message do they convey? Verses 1 – 3 can be loosely paraphrased: "Spread the word of God upon the multitudes of people in every nation, because you do not know what evil or judgment will fall upon the earth. When you have done it, don't quit, but do it again. Save as many souls as you can, because at the second coming of Jesus Christ, many ungodly people will perish like fallen trees."

Now, let's look at the specifics. Verse 1 begins with *"Cast thy bread upon the waters."* It is your bread and not someone else's. Where do you get this bread that doesn't mold, and that you may cast and find it again after many days? Jesus quizzed Philip in *John 6:5, "When Jesus then lifted up his eyes, and saw a great company come unto him, he saith unto Philip, Whence shall we buy bread, that these may eat? (6) And this he said to prove him: for he himself knew what he would do."* Sadly, Philip failed the test by focusing on money. The correct answer is Jesus Christ, who was the living Word, and now you have the written Word. This means, you must spend time with the Bible, the eternal word of God. *1Peter 1:23 Being born again, not of corruptible seed, but of incorruptible, by the word of God, which liveth and abideth for ever.*

The Apostle Paul refers to the gospel of Jesus Christ as "my gospel" in *Romans 2:16, Romans 16:25, and 2Timothy 2:8.* Similarly, notice how "a lamb," which represents the Lord Jesus, becomes "the lamb," and finally "your lamb" in *Exodus 12:3-5.* Can you say the Bible is "my Bible," in the sense that you are in the word and the word is in you?

You are to cast or sow this bread of yours to all the people in the world. This is evangelism.

Sowing the word of God is like sowing seeds. In the course of sowing, some seeds fall by the way-side and picked off by birds. These people hear the gospel message and reject it. Some seeds fall on stony places and have very little chance of making it. These people love the gospel message and accept it, but their roots are shallow in the word of God. When trials of life hit them, they are offended and leave their faith. Some seeds fall among weeds. These people have one foot in heaven and one foot in the world. They serve two masters with divided affections. The world chokes them and makes them unproductive toward God. Some seeds land on good grounds of the heart and are fruitful toward God. Read *Matthew 13:1-23.* With a 3:1 ratio, you work hard to see a good result. Nevertheless, do not be discouraged. The word of God does not return void, even though many people will reject your message. *Isaiah 55:11 So shall my word be that goeth forth out of my mouth: it shall not return unto me void, but it shall accomplish that which I please, and it shall prosper in the thing whereto I sent it.* Nothing is lost; God promises you will find His word again—*"for thou shalt find it after many days."* It may not be soon, but you will definitely find it. *1Peter 1:25 But the word of the Lord endureth for ever. And this is the word which by the gospel is preached unto you.* Read *Psalms 126:6.*

Also, sowing the word of God is not a localized or one-time effort. While you evangelize the word among family, friends, and your community, you also need to develop a world vision for getting the gospel to the four corners of the earth. Partner with faithful missionaries in getting the word out. And when you have done it, don't quit; find new fields to sow.

You are also to *"give a portion to seven, and also to eight."* This is breaking bread and rightly dividing the word of truth. It is discipleship. Teach new believers the fundamentals of the faith and the principles of Christ.

Do so with a sense of urgency because of God's impending judgment on sinners—*"for thou knowest not what evil shall be upon the earth."* God's judgment is certain to come, and many people will perish.

God's judgment on sinners will come as a downpour from heavy clouds upon the earth. But we do not know when the clouds will be full of rain. All we know is that when they are juicy, they will surely empty themselves upon the earth. It is just a matter of time. Likewise, we don't know when the judgment will come, but we are certain that it will come.

God's judgment on sinners will also come as a raging tempest that uproots and topples trees. But we do not know when the violent windy storm will come or the way of the wind. All we know and see is the aftermath of the storm. Whichever way the trees fall, they lay as evidence of the storm.

Ecclesiastes 11:4 He that observeth the wind shall not sow; and he that regardeth the clouds shall not reap. (5) As thou knowest not

what is the way of the spirit, nor how the bones do grow in the womb of her that is with child: even so thou knowest not the works of God who maketh all. (6) In the morning sow thy seed, and in the evening withhold not thine hand: for thou knowest not whether shall prosper, either this or that, or whether they both shall be alike good.

Verses 4 thru 6 above can be outlined as follows:

- The recklessness of not sowing – verse 4.
- The reasons for sowing – verse 5.
- The rules for sowing – verse 6.

Put away the farmer's almanac. Don't observe the weather. Fear neither the wind nor the clouds nor the winter's chilling breeze, but sow in faith. God's spiritual almanac says, "Good to sow and reap anytime, any day, anywhere, any condition." Some believers rely on their own wisdom and observe the wrong things. By observing the wind (anything that negates the effort of sowing), they become fearful and hold back from sowing, and by observing the clouds (anything that negates the effort of reaping), they decide to stay home and not reap. They act like they know what's going to happen, as in the way a tree will fall on a windy day.

In truth, this is God's business, so don't pretend to know the outcome of things. Some Christians are prejudiced in that they feel it is not worth their time and effort to witness to certain people.

There are four things that we don't know according to verses 5 and 6 above. We must admit we don't know the way of the Spirit in preparing people for salvation. The way of the Spirit is likened to the way of the wind in *John 3:7, "Marvel not that I said unto thee, Ye must be born again. (8) The wind bloweth where it listeth, and thou hearest the sound thereof, but canst not tell whence it cometh, and whither it goeth: so is every one that is born of the Spirit."*

We don't know how bones develop and grow in the womb. All we know is that when a baby is born, the bones are there.

Since the way God works is a mystery to us, we should simply trust and obey what He says. *Proverbs 23:4b Cease from thine own wisdom. Proverbs 3:5 Trust in the LORD with all thine heart; and lean not unto thine own understanding.*

We must realize that there is a spiritual operation happening behind the scenes and that we are laborers together with God (*1Corinthians 3:9*). The increase and fruit from the operation, however, are up to God. *1Corinthians 3:6 I have planted, Apollos watered; but God gave the increase. (7) So then neither is he that planteth any thing, neither he that watereth; but God that giveth the increase.*

God says, "*In the morning sow thy seed, and in the evening withhold not thine hand.*" The morning and evening not only refer to the times of day, but also to the seasons of life. We are to sow the word of God in our youth, as well as in the sun-setting years of our lives. *Psalms 92:12 The righteous shall flourish like the palm tree: he shall grow like a cedar in Lebanon. (13) Those that be planted in the house of the LORD shall flourish in the courts of our God. (14) They shall still bring forth fruit in old age; they shall be fat and flourishing.* We also don't need to attain the level of Bible teacher before sowing the word of God. All believers must be able to share their personal testimony of salvation. (If you don't have a salvation testimony, you are not saved. You may have a religion or religious experience, but not a personal relationship with Christ.)

We are to be diligent in sowing and not to withhold our hands, because we know not which will bear fruit—the seeds sown in the morning or in the evening, or both. This is success through quantity and repetition. When we have witnessed to seven people, witness also to the eighth.

Go online and listen to the hymn "Bringing in the sheaves" by Knowles Shaw.

> Sowing in the morning, sowing seeds of kindness,
> Sowing in the noontide and the dewy eve;
> Waiting for the harvest, and the time of reaping,
> We shall come rejoicing, bringing in the sheaves.
>
> Chorus:
> Bringing in the sheaves, bringing in the sheaves,
> We shall come rejoicing, bringing in the sheaves;
> Bringing in the sheaves, bringing in the sheaves,
> We shall come rejoicing, bringing in the sheaves.
>
> Sowing in the sunshine, sowing in the shadows,
> Fearing neither clouds nor winter's chilling breeze;
> By and by the harvest, and the labor ended,
> We shall come rejoicing, bringing in the sheaves.
>
> Going forth with weeping, sowing for the Master,
> Tho' the loss sustained our spirit often grieves;
> When our weeping's over, He will bid us welcome,
> We shall come rejoicing, bringing in the sheaves.

Ecclesiastes 11:7 Truly the light is sweet, and a pleasant thing it is for the eyes to behold the sun: (8) But if a man live many years, and rejoice in them all; yet let him remember the days of darkness; for they shall be many. All that cometh is vanity.

In the close of his sermon, Solomon addresses both mature and young people, with the bulk of his admonition toward the latter. (Compare this to *1John 2:13, "I write unto you, fathers, because ye have known him that is from the beginning. I write unto you, young men, because ye have overcome the wicked one. I write unto you, little children, because ye have known the Father."*) The common word in his admonition is "remember."

It is good to be alive and see the sun and enjoy the beautiful days of blue sky and white puffy clouds. Sunlight is so pleasurable that heathens all over the world build temples to worship the sun.

Yet don't get carried away with the good days or good life, because they are finite. We will die someday and our eyes will cease to see the light of day. The darkness of death will shroud our bodies in the grave. And if the Lord delays His return, the joyless days of darkness will be many, perhaps longer than our earthly existence.

The counsel for mature people is to *"remember the days of darkness"* that shall come. *Job 10:20 Are not my days few? cease then, and let me alone, that I may take comfort a little, (21) Before I go whence I shall not return, even to the land of darkness and the shadow of death; (22) A land of darkness, as darkness itself; and of the shadow of death, without any order, and where the light is as darkness.* Keeping death at the forefront of our mind, especially during the sweetness of life when everything goes our way, helps to set a right perspective on life. Don't go to the grave without dutifully fulfilling the Great Commission—sowing the word of God and reaping souls for His kingdom. In the grave, it is too late for ministry work—*"All that cometh is vanity."* *Psalms 88:10 Wilt thou shew wonders to the dead? shall the dead arise and praise thee? Selah. (11) Shall thy lovingkindness be declared in the grave? or thy faithfulness in destruction? (12) Shall thy wonders be known in the dark? and thy righteousness in the land of forgetfulness? (13) But unto thee have I cried, O LORD; and in the morning shall my prayer prevent thee.*

Physical light is sweet, but the spiritual light of life is much sweeter. *John 8:12 Then spake Jesus again unto them, saying, I am the light of the world: he that followeth me shall not walk in darkness, but shall have the light of life.* One of these days, our eyes will see the real Sun. *Malachi 4:2 But unto you that fear my name shall the <u>Sun</u> of righteousness arise with healing in his wings; and ye* *shall go forth, and grow up as calves of the stall.* That's all that matters, because nothing of this world satisfies. It is all vanity.

Ecclesiastes 11:9 Rejoice, O young man, in thy youth; and let thy heart cheer thee in the days of thy youth, and walk in the ways of thine heart, and in the sight of thine eyes: but know thou, that for all these things God will bring thee into judgment. (10) Therefore remove sorrow from thy heart, and put away evil from thy flesh: for childhood and youth are vanity.

Hello young people. (The phrase *"young man"* in verse 9 covers a period of life from boyhood to manhood—before the hair turns grey.) Don't misread verse 9, because it is sarcasm. The recommendation to walk after your heart and sight is as sarcastic as the "eat, drink, and be merry" recommendation for self-serving people in *Ecclesiastes 2:24, Ecclesiastes 3:13, Ecclesiastes 5:18, Ecclesiastes 8:15,* and *Ecclesiastes 9:7.*

Below are the guidelines for living an enjoyable and happy life in the days of youth:

- Let your enjoyment be tempered by the fact that God is always watching and will hold you accountable for all your actions. There are lines you shouldn't cross in order to enjoy life. Be smart not to provoke God to rain on your party.

  I know you think this kind of enjoyment is no fun. I minister at a juvenile detention center where the boys play basketball under the watchful eyes of the guards. They get to enjoy the game as long as they play by the rules. The moment someone gets out of line, the guards move in, the game ends, and everyone returns to their cell.

Your enjoyments must be lawful and biblical, otherwise, the authorities and God will hunt you down, and life will not be fun. Remember, you are always being watched.

- The time of youth is characterized by being high on passion, low on discretion—quick to anger, combative, and addicted to youthful lusts. Put away anger and sin, because they are enemies to your enjoyment. Wouldn't you rather be having fun than be angry? Read *James 1:19-21, 2Timothy 2:22.*

- Childhood and youth are vanity; the time is very short. *Ecclesiastes 11:9* refers to it as *"days of thy youth."* To maximize enjoyment, you must do it the right way. Don't get into trouble with God and human authorities.

  The youths at the juvenile detention center that I minister to are in for several months, some for more than a year. The timeout is no fun and eats away their time of youth. Many are repeat offenders.

The above is a tall order for rebellious youths who never learn to submit to authority (parents, teachers, pastors, and the word of God) or grow up wild in dysfunctional families. The days of their youth are tumultuous and full of drama.

Ecclesiastes 12:1 Remember now thy Creator in the days of thy youth, while the evil days come not, nor the years draw nigh, when thou shalt say, I have no pleasure in them;

Don't waste your youth in carnal pleasures and sensual gratifications, walking after the ways of your heart and eyes. Rather, serve God. Get a job, learn the Bible, and be discipled; save some money, and perhaps take the gospel to far flung places, even to dangerous places that are hostile to Christianity. Now that's real excitement and an adrenaline rush compared to meaningless computer games. (Three times have I preached the gospel in India in areas that are known to kill Christians.) Which is better, a life wasted in vanity or a life spent for God?

Ecclesiastes 12:1-7 divides beautifully into three sections:

1. Remember and serve God in the days of your youth – *Ecclesiastes 12:1.*
2. Remember and serve God before you circle the drain – *Ecclesiastes 12:2-5.*
3. Remember and serve God before you die – *Ecclesiastes 12:6-7.*

Remember your Creator-creature relationship. You don't exist from nothing, and the chimpanzee is not your closest relative. God wants you to enter into a relationship with His Son Jesus Christ. It begins with acknowledging you are a sinner and that the wages of your sin is death. By faith, you accept the gift of God, which is eternal life through Jesus Christ. This can be done through a sincere prayer—confess Jesus as Lord with your mouth, and with your heart believe that God raised Him from the dead. *Romans 3:23 For all have sinned, and come short of the glory of God. Romans 6:23 For the wages of sin is death; but the gift of God is eternal life through Jesus Christ our Lord. Romans 10:9 That if thou shalt confess with thy mouth the Lord Jesus, and shalt believe in thine heart that God hath raised him from the dead, thou shalt be saved. (10) For with the heart man believeth unto righteousness; and with the mouth confession is made unto salvation.*

Remember your Creator for the reason of your existence. He created you on purpose to glorify Him. You don't exist to live for self. *Revelation 4:11 Thou art worthy, O Lord, to receive glory and honour and power: for thou hast created all things, and for thy pleasure they are and were created. Colossians 1:16 For by him were all things created, that are in heaven, and that are in earth, visible and invisible, whether they be thrones, or dominions, or principalities, or powers: all things were created by him, and for him: (17) And he is before all things, and by him all things consist.* Read *Psalms 100:3.*

Remember your Creator for your duty to Him. This is so that you can chart the right course and equip yourself for the duty, which includes loving Him and advancing His gospel. *Mark 12:30 And thou shalt love the Lord thy God with all thy heart, and with all thy soul, and with all thy mind, and with all thy strength: this is the first commandment.* Read *Deuteronomy 6:5, Deuteronomy 11:1, Joshua 23:11, Matthew 22:37, Luke 10:27. Matthew 28: 19 Go ye therefore, and teach all nations, baptizing them in the name of the Father, and of the Son, and of the Holy Ghost: (20) Teaching them to observe all things whatsoever I have commanded you: and, lo, I am with you alway, even unto the end of the world. Amen.*

Remember your Creator because you will drift. By setting God as the lighthouse or point of reference, you will know how far you have drifted and be able to find your way back. *Proverbs22:28 Remove not the ancient landmark, which thy fathers have set.*

Remember your Creator while there is hope for you. *Proverbs 19:18 Chasten thy son while there is hope, and let not thy soul spare for his crying.* The time to bend a tree is when it is young. Once the narrow window of opportunity closes, you are hardened like an established tree. It is your parents' job to bend you while you are young. *Proverbs 22:6 Train up a child in the way he should go: and when he is old, he will not depart from it.* If your parents failed in this job, God will take over the task and bend you. You may crack, snap, and break. Trust me, it is not fun. *Proverbs 29:1 He, that being often reproved hardeneth his neck, shall suddenly be destroyed, and that without remedy.*

The best timeframe to remember your Creator is *"in the days of thy youth."*

- Before the affliction of evil days when God visits your sins. If you don't remember the Creator as mentioned above, you will rack up sins, and the season of reckoning will bring miseries. *Psalms 25:7 Remember not the sins of my youth, nor my transgressions: according to thy mercy remember thou me for thy goodness' sake, O LORD.*

- Before *"the years draw nigh"* or old age, when you are crippled, constrained, and debilitating pains are your closest companions. You will be so miserable that you will have no pleasure in living. Whereas right now, you have no pleasure in serving.

Ecclesiastes 12:2 While the sun, or the light, or the moon, or the stars, be not darkened, nor the clouds return after the rain: (3) In the day when the keepers of the house shall tremble, and the strong men shall bow themselves, and the grinders cease because they are few, and those that look out of the windows be darkened, (4) And the doors shall be shut in the streets, when the sound of the grinding is low, and he shall rise up at the voice of the bird, and all the daughters of musick shall be brought low; (5) Also when they shall be afraid of that which is high, and fears shall be in the way, and the almond tree shall flourish, and the grasshopper shall be a burden, and desire shall fail: because man goeth to his long home, and the mourners go about the streets:

The above verses are a finely crafted figurative description of infirmities associated with old age. Compare this passage of scripture with another elegantly shaped figurative description of a beautiful woman, by the same author in *The Song of Solomon 7:1-6.*

The above verses have been variously interpreted. Even so, do not lose the important message, which is to remember the Creator and serve Him before you circle the drain, when death approaches like a terrifying storm with no end in sight. As soon as one storm passes, dark rain clouds immediately redevelop.

You will wake up one day realizing that your body is not what it used to be. You are not as quick and agile, and pains begin to emerge. Your organs and functions begin to decay, and there will be no doubt that your sun is setting. The infirmities make you miserable and impair your ability to serve God.

- Serve God before your glory turns to gloom; before your cognitive function fails; before brain diseases like Alzheimer's or dementia cause you to lose your marbles – *"While the sun, or the light, or the moon, or the stars, be not darkened."*

- Serve God before your physical strength turns sloppy.
  o Before the neurodegenerative brain disorder known as Parkinson's disease destroys your nervous system and causes your hands and legs (keepers of the house) to tremble uncontrollably – *"In the day when the keepers of the house shall tremble."*
  o Before osteoporosis sets in and your body can no longer do and bear the work of ministry – *"the strong men shall bow themselves."* Strong men bow themselves unwillingly.
  o Before gingivitis or periodontitis destroys gum tissues and bones, taking away your teeth and the ability to chow down – *"the grinders cease because they are few."* Grinders refer to molar teeth. The work of ministry is tough; you have to eat for strength.
  o Before cataracts blur your vision – *"those that look out of the windows be darkened."* It's hard to be

independent and go places to share the gospel when you can't see your way.

- Serve God before your enjoyment turns to embarrassment.
  - o Before you are unable to enjoy solid food – *"And the doors shall be shut in the streets, when the sound of the grinding is low."* Due to the lack of teeth, the lips (doors) must be shut tight, otherwise, food will drop out. *Job 41:14 Who can open the doors of his face? his teeth are terrible round about.*
  - o Before you lose restful sleep due to various pains – *"he shall rise up at the voice of the bird." Job 7:4 When I lie down, I say, When shall I arise, and the night be gone? and I am full of tossings to and fro unto the dawning of the day.*
  - o Before you struggle to enunciate words or lose your hearing – *"all the daughters of musick shall be brought low."* It is hard to share the gospel with people when you struggle to speak and hear clearly. *2Samuel 19:35 I am this day fourscore years old: and can I discern between good and evil? can thy servant taste what I eat or what I drink? can I hear any more the voice of singing men and singing women? wherefore then should thy servant be yet a burden unto my lord the king?*

- Serve God before your stability turns to shakiness, when you are afraid of falling and the possibility of breaking bones – *"Also when they shall be afraid of that which is high, and fears shall be in the way."*

- Serve God before your desire turns to distaste – *"the almond tree shall flourish, and the grasshopper shall be a burden, and desire shall fail."*

- o Asians and middle Easterners go nuts for almonds. When almond trees blossom in late February and early March, they paint the entire grove white against the blue sky, setting happy expectations for delicious fruit. The white blossoms represent the hoary heads of old age. The distresses associated with decrepit old age kill appetites and desires.
- o Grasshoppers are also a delicacy in the East. But again, the distresses of old age cause such a delicacy to not sit well in the stomach.

- Serve God before you go from the old folks' home to the long home (the grave) — *"man goeth to his long home, and the mourners go about the streets."* Don't be a spiritually fruitless old person, because the next phase in life is death. *Job 17:13 If I wait, the grave is mine house: I have made my bed in the darkness. Job 30:23 For I know that thou wilt bring me to death, and to the house appointed for all living.* In Eastern cultures, living relatives hire professional mourners to bemoan the departure of the dead. (When my grandpa died, my dad hired professional mourners. It was quite a show.) Read *Mark 5:35-39.*

Ecclesiastes 12:6 Or ever the silver cord be loosed, or the golden bowl be broken, or the pitcher be broken at the fountain, or the wheel broken at the cistern. (7) Then shall the dust return to the earth as it was: and the spirit shall return unto God who gave it.

Finally, death arrives to claim its victim. Pictured in verse 6 above are two metaphors of death:

- Life is snuffed out like a hanging lamp that is dashed down and broken. In old Eastern countries, lamps are hung from ceilings and pillars by cords of silk and silver interwoven. When the cord snaps, the lamp comes crashing down. As to the representation of this metaphor to the human body, the golden bowl may be the head, and the silver cord may be the spinal marrow, which descends like a cord from the brain through the neck. The cause of death may be stroke or bone marrow cancer. (There are various thoughts for what the objects in verse 6 represent. Some people take the silver cord to be the life thread connecting the physical and spiritual bodies. Since the phrases "silver cord" and "golden bowl" occur only once in the Bible, we should not be dogmatic about it.)

In the Bible, silver and gold represent the price of redemption and the deity of Christ respectively. A person without a personal relationship with Jesus Christ is an unredeemed and godless person who is spiritually dead. It is as if the person's silver cord is disconnected from the source of life, and the individual's golden bowl is broken.

- Life is snuffed out because the pitcher and wheel are broken and can no longer supply life-sustaining water. The human heart is a good representation of this metaphor, as it is both a fountain and a cistern. The pitcher and the fountain are the left ventricle of the heart that is responsible for collecting oxygenated blood from the lungs and pumping the blood to tissues all over the body. The wheel and the cistern are the right ventricle of the heart that is responsible for collecting oxygen-depleted blood from tissues and pumping the blood to the lungs. Cardiac arrest may be the cause of death in this illustration. (Again, we should not be dogmatic about the representations.)

Spiritually, this portrays a person who rejects Christ and has no access to the living water. This person is also spiritually dead. *Jeremiah 2:13 For my people have committed two evils; they have forsaken me the fountain of living waters, and hewed them out cisterns, broken cisterns, that can hold no water. John 4:10 Jesus answered and said unto her, If thou knewest the gift of God, and who it is that saith to thee, Give me to drink; thou wouldest have asked of him, and he would have given thee living water.*

Death is a great leveler; the end result is always the same. Without the spirit, the body decomposes to its base material—*"for dust thou art, and unto dust shalt thou return." Ecclesiastes 3:20 All go unto one place; all are of the dust, and all turn to dust again.* The human spirit returns to God. *Ecclesiastes 8:8 There is no man that hath power over the spirit to retain the spirit; neither hath he power in the day of death: and there is no discharge in that war; neither shall wickedness deliver those that are given to it.*

The worst part about death is that one has to face God and His judgment. *Hebrews 9:27 And as it is appointed unto men once to die, but after this the judgment.* Make sure you are right with God through a relationship with His Son Jesus Christ. *1John 5:12 He that hath the Son hath life; and he that hath not the Son of God hath not life.* Also make sure you have spiritual fruit to show at the Judgment Seat of Christ. Don't wake up one day realizing that you have wasted your life by living for self.

Go online and listen to the hymn "Saved by grace" by Frances J. Crosby and George C. Stebbins.

Someday the silver cord will break,
And I no more as now shall sing;
But, oh, the joy when I shall wake
Within the palace of the King!

Chorus:
And I shall see Him face to face,
And tell the story—Saved by grace.
And I shall see Him face to face,
And tell the story—Saved by grace.

Someday my earthly house will fall;
I cannot tell how soon 'twill be;
But this I know—my All in All
Has now a place in heav'n for me.

Someday, when fades the golden sun
Beneath the rosy tinted west,
My blessed Lord will say, "Well done!"
And I shall enter into rest.

Someday: till then I'll watch and wait,
My lamp all trimmed and burning bright,
That when my Savior opens the gate,
My soul to Him may take its flight.

I will do you disservice if I don't re-plow *Ecclesiastes 12:2-5* to show the prophecy of the second coming of the Lord Jesus Christ in it. These verses are the grand finale of the best fireworks show.

- *Ecclesiastes 12:2-3* talks about the imminent terrifying day of darkness.
  Joel 2:1 Blow ye the trumpet in Zion, and sound an alarm in my holy mountain: <u>let all the inhabitants of the land tremble: for the day of the LORD cometh</u>, for it is nigh at hand; (2) <u>A day of darkness and of gloominess, a day of clouds and of thick darkness</u>, as the morning spread upon the mountains: a great people and a strong; there hath not been ever the like, neither shall be any more after it, even to the years of many generations. (3) A fire devoureth before them; and behind them a flame

burneth: the land is as the garden of Eden before them, and behind them a desolate wilderness; yea, and nothing shall escape them. (4) The appearance of them is as the appearance of horses; and as horsemen, so shall they run. (5) Like the noise of chariots on the tops of mountains shall they leap, like the noise of a flame of fire that devoureth the stubble, as a strong people set in battle array. (6) Before their face the people shall be much pained: all faces shall gather blackness. (7) They shall run like mighty men; they shall climb the wall like men of war; and they shall march every one on his ways, and they shall not break their ranks: (8) Neither shall one thrust another; they shall walk every one in his path: and when they fall upon the sword, they shall not be wounded. (9) They shall run to and fro in the city; they shall run upon the wall, they shall climb up upon the houses; they shall enter in at the windows like a thief. (10) The earth shall quake before them; the heavens shall tremble: the sun and the moon shall be dark, and the stars shall withdraw their shining: (11) And the LORD shall utter his voice before his army: for his camp is very great: for he is strong that executeth his word: for the day of the LORD is great and very terrible; and who can abide it? ... (31) The sun shall be turned into darkness, and the moon into blood, before the great and the terrible day of the LORD come.

Joel 3:14 Multitudes, multitudes in the valley of decision: for the day of the LORD is near in the valley of decision. (15) The sun and the moon shall be darkened, and the stars shall withdraw their shining. (16) The LORD also shall roar out of Zion, and utter his voice from Jerusalem; and the heavens and the earth shall shake: but the LORD will be the hope of his people, and the strength of the children of Israel.

Zephaniah 1:14 The great day of the LORD is near, it is near, and hasteth greatly, even the voice of the day of the LORD: the mighty man shall cry there bitterly. (15) That day is a day of wrath, a day of trouble and distress, a day of wasteness and desolation, a day of darkness and gloominess, a day of clouds and thick darkness, (16) A day of the trumpet and alarm against the fenced cities, and against the high towers. (17) And I will bring distress upon men, that they shall walk like blind men, because they have sinned against the LORD: and their blood shall be poured out as dust, and their flesh as the dung.

- The phrase, *"clouds return after the rain"* in *Ecclesiastes 12:2* refers to the "latter rain," which signifies the end of the Great Tribulation and the second coming of the Lord Jesus Christ. *James 5:7 Be patient therefore, brethren, unto the coming of the Lord. Behold, the husbandman waiteth for the precious fruit of the earth, and hath long patience for it, until he receive the early and latter rain. Proverbs 16:15 In the light of the king's countenance is life; and his favour is as a cloud of the latter rain.*

- Notice the change in pronoun to "he" in *Ecclesiastes 12:4*. Who is "he?" This is the Lord Jesus Christ.

- *Ecclesiastes 12:4-5* talks about people fearful of what is coming down from on high. *Zechariah 14:4 And his feet shall stand in that day upon the mount of Olives, which is before Jerusalem on the east, and the mount of Olives shall cleave in the midst thereof toward the east and toward the west, and there shall be a very great valley; and half of the mountain shall remove toward the north, and half of it toward the south.*

- The time of the second coming of Christ may be in the early spring, when the almond trees flourish, according to *Ecclesiastes 12:5*. This is also in line with the timing of the latter rain. *Joel 2:23 Be glad then, ye children of Zion, and rejoice in the LORD your God: for he hath given you the former rain moderately, and he will cause to come down for you the rain, the former rain, and the latter rain in the first month.* The Jewish first month is Nisan, which corresponds to March – April. (Don't confuse the second coming of the Lord Jesus Christ with the rapture of the church. At the rapture, the Lord meets His believers in the air. His feet do not touch the ground. At His second coming, which is seven years after the rapture of the church, the Lord's feet touch down on the Mount of Olives and split the mountain.)

Ecclesiastes 12:8 Vanity of vanities, saith the preacher; all is vanity.

With this epilogue, we have come full circle. God's words are the same in the beginning and in the end. This world is the vanity of vanities. It has no real happiness and nothing to satisfy the soul. It is vanity of the worst kind in disguise. Solomon, the wisest and richest person who ever lived, proved it philosophically and empirically through extensive research and experience. And we should be able to say "Amen," because we also have experienced vanity firsthand by misplacing our hope and affections on the things of the world.

In case you are not convinced, search the internet for "famous faces of depression" and "famous faces of suicide." How many people do you recognize? What do you have that they did not—success, fame, fortune, good looks, or power? The fact that their methods for happiness did not work doesn't raise a red flag or two? What makes you the exception to the rule?

Are you done chasing after happiness that doesn't exist? Would you now set your affections on things above and serve God? *Colossians 3:1 If ye then be risen with Christ, seek those things which are above, where Christ sitteth on the right hand of God. (2) Set your affection on things above, not on things on the earth. (3) For ye are dead, and your life is hid with Christ in God.*

Ecclesiastes 12:9 And moreover, because the preacher was wise, he still taught the people knowledge; yea, he gave good heed, and sought out, and set in order many proverbs.

The verse begins with *"And moreover,"* which means above all that is said, now pay special attention as this is the prelude to the central conclusion of the royal sermon. The focus now returns to the preacher and his words.

We have here a wise preacher, a royal preacher, a faithful and diligent teacher (rabbi), an author, and a king who disregarded his kingship. In this sense, Solomon is a type of Christ. But Solomon as a repentant preacher, did not let his past sins prevent him from exercising his gifts and fulfilling his duty to God. He continued to teach knowledge to common people. *Proverbs 24:16 For a just man falleth seven times, and riseth up again: but the wicked shall fall into mischief.* He was diligent and meticulous in preparing his teachings, painstakingly searching out and arranging in order many proverbs. (When I studied the book of Proverbs as a young Christian, I was not impressed, because the author seemed to be a scatterbrain. I wanted to group the verses into their respective categories, such as fools, wise, raising children, managing wealth, etc. While that was alright, I failed to realize that the verses were deliberately arranged, as precious stones set by a master gem setter. A piece of jewelry composed of stones of various kinds, colors, and sizes is beautiful.)

Many of us can identify with Solomon as we also have departed from and disappointed the Lord. Praise God for His grace that is greater than all our sins. When we repent of our sins, we should attend to the Father's business again. Let not our sins and shame beat us down and hold us back from fulfilling our duty to God.

We also learn from Solomon that an investment in the word of God is the best investment, as it continues to educate and transform people long after we are gone. Solomon died around 931 B.C. and continues to teach people knowledge till this day. Did you know that Charles Spurgeon, D.L. Moody, and G. Campbell Morgan are still preaching and teaching today, even though they are dead? Think about the people who have invested the word of God in you. Are you investing the word of God in the lives of others?

Ecclesiastes 12:10 The preacher sought to find out acceptable words: and that which was written was upright, even words of truth. (11) The words of the wise are as goads, and as nails fastened by the masters of assemblies, which are given from one shepherd. (12) And further, by these, my son, be admonished: of making many books there is no end; and much study is a weariness of the flesh.

Solomon composed his writings with a great deal of labor and care as he searched for acceptable words, not so that he could please his readers, but that he might please God. He labored for the words of truth. (Acceptable words are the written words of truth.)

Verses 10 thru 12 may be outlined as follows:

- Written words – verse 10.
- Functional words – verse 11.
- Beneficial words – verse 12.

Happiness is framed by the written word of God. The book of Ecclesiastes begins with *"The words of the Preacher,"* and ends with *"The preacher sought to find out acceptable words."* *Hebrews 11:3 Through faith we understand that the worlds were framed by the word of God, so that things which are seen were not made of things which do appear.*

There is no happiness outside of the written word of God, which was personified by Jesus Christ. *John 1:1 In the beginning was the Word, and the Word was with God, and the Word was God. (14) And the Word was made flesh, and dwelt among us, (and we beheld his glory, the glory as of the only begotten of the Father,) full of grace and truth.* True happiness lies in a personal relationship with the Christ of Christianity and not in a religion or a religious banner.

The written words are upright and truth. *John 17:17 Sanctify them through thy truth: thy word is truth.* They are absolutely reliable and certain. We can take them to the bank. *Proverbs 22:20 Have not I written to thee excellent things in counsels and knowledge, (21) That I might make thee know the certainty of the words of truth; that thou mightest answer the words of truth to them that send unto thee?*

The written words are functional words of wisdom. They function as goads that drive and urge us forward to duty, and as nails or stakes that fasten us to the foundation (Jesus Christ) and to the body of Christ (the church), that we may interoperate with other believers. *1Corinthians 3:11 For other foundation can no man lay than that is laid, which is Jesus Christ. Ephesians 4:16 From whom the whole body fitly joined together and compacted by that which every joint supplieth, according to the effectual working in the measure of every part, maketh increase of the body unto the edifying of itself in love.* God supplies masters of assemblies to help build up and mature the body of Christ. *Ephesians 4:11 And he gave some, apostles; and some, prophets; and some, evangelists; and some, pastors and teachers; (12) For the perfecting of the saints, for the work of the ministry, for the edifying of the body of Christ: (13) Till we all come in the unity of the faith, and of the knowledge of the Son of God, unto a perfect man, unto the measure of the stature of the fulness of Christ: (14) That we henceforth be no more children, tossed to and fro, and carried about with every wind of doctrine, by the sleight of men, and cunning craftiness, whereby they lie in wait to deceive; (15) But speaking the truth in love, may grow up into him in all things, which is the head, even Christ.*

The written words emanate from one Shepherd, who is Jesus Christ. *John 10:14 I am the good shepherd, and know my sheep, and am known of mine. (15) As the Father knoweth me, even so know I the Father: and I lay down my life for the sheep. (16) And other sheep I have, which are not of this fold: them also I must bring, and they shall hear my voice; and there shall be one fold, and one shepherd.*

The written words are beneficial words of admonition, affectionately addressed to the sons of God. (This is the only place the phrase "my son" appears in the book of Ecclesiastes.) The book is divinely inspired and is the definitive book on happiness. By it, we clearly see this world for what it really is—vanity of vanities. This helps us to release the world from our hearts, recalibrate our affections on things that matter, and live a meaningful life. We are hereby notified that there is no need to write new books or conduct new studies on happiness. The book of Ecclesiastes is all that we need to live a happy life under the sun. You may have bought secular books and programs that took you down futile paths in search of happiness. *2Timothy 3:7 Ever learning, and never able to come to the knowledge of the truth.* The authors can't even figure out where humans come from, much less lead you to true happiness. Don't waste your time and money on them. It is also a weariness of flesh to keep up with their nonsense.

Ecclesiastes 12:13 Let us hear the conclusion of the whole matter: Fear God, and keep his commandments: for this is the whole duty of man. (14) For God shall bring every work into judgment, with every secret thing, whether it be good, or whether it be evil.

We are hereby invited to hear the conclusion of the matter concerning the true happiness of mankind, and the answer to, *"What was that good for the sons of men, which they should do under the heaven all the days of their life?"* And not just casual hearing, but to hear attentively, to receive whole heartedly, and to obey willingly the information provided. *Proverbs 4:10a Hear, O my son, and receive my sayings. Proverbs 23:19 Hear thou, my son, and be wise, and guide thine heart in the way.* Solomon paid dearly to give us this conclusion, and we must not file it away and do nothing with it.

The conclusion: To be happy is to fear God, and keep His commandments.

Notice the comma after *"fear God?"* The message changes drastically with the comma. It means we must first learn to fear God before we can properly keep His commandments.

An example of the fear of God is in the story of Abraham offering up Isaac in *Genesis 22*. God said to Abraham, *"Take now thy son, thine only son Isaac, whom thou lovest, and get thee into the land of Moriah; and offer him there for a burnt offering upon one of the mountains which I will tell thee of."* Abraham obeyed God, and was about to slay Isaac before God stopped him: *"Lay not thine hand upon the lad, neither do thou any thing unto him: for now I know that thou fearest God, seeing thou hast not withheld thy son, thine only son from me."* Notice that only a perfect fear of God can result in complete obedience to His words.

Our fear of God must be learned from the Bible. *Isaiah 29:13 Wherefore the Lord said, Forasmuch as this people draw near me with their mouth, and with their lips do honour me, but have* removed their heart far from me, and their fear toward me is taught by the precept of men. *Psalms 34:11* says, *"Come, ye children, hearken unto me: I will teach you the fear of the LORD."* Read *Psalms 34, Proverbs 2, Job 28:28, Psalms 111:10, Proverbs 1:7, Proverbs 8:13, Proverbs 9:10, Proverbs 14:27, Proverbs 15:33, Proverbs 16:6.*

Psalms 89:7 says, *"God is greatly to be feared in the assembly of the saints, and to be had in reverence of all them that are about him."* Yet this is not the crippling fear that sends a person into a corner curled up in the fetal position. This fear prevents us from living for self and moves us to depart from evil, keep His commandments, and fulfill our duty to Him. It results in reverence for His majesty and obedience to His words. We just learned above that the written words are as goads. *Deuteronomy 10:12 And now, Israel, what doth the LORD thy God require of thee, but to fear the LORD thy God, to walk in all his ways, and to love him, and to serve the LORD thy God with all thy heart and with all thy soul.* Notice "fear" goes before "walk," "love," and "serve.

An improper fear of God causes people to be flippant with Him and His commandments. Yes, He is our heavenly Father, but He is first and foremost God—*"In the beginning God."*

An improper fear of God results in an imperfect duty with eternal consequences. What we do for God and His kingdom in our lifetime will determine our eternal state in heaven. God will reward us according to our deeds. Every work, including those done in secret, will be brought into account at the Judgment Seat of Christ. *1Corinthians 3:13 Every man's work shall be made manifest: for the day shall declare it, because it shall be revealed by fire; and the fire shall try every man's work of what sort it is. (14) If any man's work abide which he hath built thereupon, he shall receive a reward. (15) If any man's work shall be burned, he shall suffer loss: but he himself shall be saved; yet so as by fire.*

We definitely do not want to show up empty handed at the Judgment Seat. This is dereliction of duty and would be equivalent to an "F" on a scorecard. We also do not want to bring unsatisfactory results that are equivalent to a "B" or "C," because we lived mostly for ourselves and served God with our leftovers. We have one chance—one lifetime and one platform (the world) to demonstrate our gratitude for His great salvation and our obedience to His commandments.

Are you able to articulate the gospel and lead a lost person to the Lord? Are you willing and able to invest the word of God in another believer? If not, it is high time to do something about it. May God give you the wisdom to recognize that He is to be feared and is worth being right with. May God bless you and make you spiritually fruitful.

Appendix A – How to Accept Jesus Christ as Lord and Savior

There's a reason for the world-wide epidemic of unhappiness leading to depression and suicidal thoughts. God created each and every one of us to have a relationship with Him. He has always wanted our love and devotion. But that is the furthest thing from our minds.

Rather than live a God-focused life, we all pursue ourselves and succumb to the thinking of the world (under the sun), where we will never find happiness.

Proverbs 3:13 says, *"Happy is the man that findeth wisdom, and the man that getteth understanding."* This wisdom and understanding starts with a personal relationship with Jesus as Lord and Savior. To get this relationship, we must start at the beginning. We must be born again. *John 3:3 Jesus answered and said unto him, Verily, verily, I say unto thee, Except a man be born again, he cannot see the kingdom of God.*

The path to rebirth is simple. Here are the things you must understand:

- Problem of mankind
  Sin ruined everything. Our first birth was defective. *Romans 3:23 For all have sinned, and come short of the glory of God.* Read *Romans 5:12, Psalms 51:5*. Given that we were all born with a sin nature, our natural self is not

patchable or repairable by worldly or physical means. No amount of education, religion, morality, or good works can erase sin and secure a right relationship with God. Read *Ephesians 2:8-9, Romans 11:6, Hebrews 11:6.*

- Penalty of sin
  The Bible says, *"The wages of sin is death."* Sinners who die in their sins are eternally separated from God. Their unrighteous souls will stand in judgment and be found guilty 100% of the time, and they will burn in the lake of fire for eternity. *Ezekiel 18:4 Behold, all souls are mine; as the soul of the father, so also the soul of the son is mine: the soul that sinneth, it shall die.* All unregenerated sinners will die a second death. As the faithful saying goes, "If you are born once, you will die twice; if you are born twice, you will die once." Read *Hebrews 9:27, Isaiah 64:6, John 8:23-24, Revelation 20:11-15.*

- Provision of God
  John 3:16 says, *"For God so loved the world, that he gave his only begotten Son, that whosoever believeth in him should not perish, but have everlasting life."* Salvation is God's free gift made available through Jesus Christ only. *Romans 6:23 For the wages of sin is death; but the gift of God is eternal life through Jesus Christ our Lord.*

Our greatest necessity is to be born again by the Holy Spirit of God, which is a spiritual operation through faith in Jesus Christ. The spiritual birth is distinctly different than the first birth by flesh— *"That which is born of the flesh is flesh; and that which is born of the Spirit is spirit."* (*John 3:6*) Unlike physical birth, spiritual birth is invisible. However, the evidence should be very clear.

Appendix A – How to Accept Jesus Christ as Lord and Savior

Being saved or born again is based on knowledge of the word of God combined with faith and not on feelings, good works, visions, experiences, or membership in a certain religion or denomination. Sadly, many overturn Bible truth with their feelings and experiences.

You need to know that you are a sinner bound for hell and that God loves you, sent His Son to die for your sins, and salvation is a free gift available only in Jesus Christ. *John 14:6 Jesus saith unto him, I am the way, the truth, and the life: no man cometh unto the Father, but by me.*

Salvation is a transaction—a conscious decision to exchange sin and death for forgiveness and eternal life. Be extremely careful, because many people claim to be Christians who are not Christians. Their salvation testimonies are uncertain and incorrect. Examples of false saving faith include surviving a terrible accident or near-death experience, speaking in tongues, water baptism, good works, church membership, familiarity with Jesus' stories, someone praying for them, and so on. I once asked a man if he knew the Lord. He replied, "Oh, I was baptized when I was 12." He was basing his salvation on his baptism and was living with a false hope. Just when I thought I'd heard it all, a young lady claimed to be a Christian because she prayed and God healed her sick dog.

Here is a test: If God were to ask you why He should let you into heaven, what would you say?

What is required to be born again? Accepting Jesus Christ as Lord and Savior by faith through a simple prayer with the following understanding:

- Admission of sin before Jesus Christ. Jesus is of no use to the self-righteous, just as doctors are of no use to sick people who refuse to admit they are sick. Read *Mark 2:17*. You must see yourself as lost before you can be saved.

- Understanding the penalty of sin is death.

- Realizing that only Jesus Christ can forgive sins. Read *1Timothy 2:5, John 14:6, 1John 2:23, 1John 5:11-13, Acts 4:10-12, Matthew 7:13-14.*

- Agreeing that God's salvation is a free gift and not a loan or debt that should be repaid through good works. All that is necessary is to simply receive the gift with a sincere prayer and a believing heart. A gift is free to the recipient. The giver is the one who pays the price. God's salvation is a free gift that is dearly paid for by Christ's blood shed on the cross.

- Accepting Jesus Christ as Lord and Savior by faith through a simple prayer. *Romans 10:9 That if thou shalt confess with thy mouth the Lord Jesus, and shalt believe in thine heart that God hath raised him from the dead, thou shalt be saved. (10) For with the heart man believeth unto righteousness; and with the mouth confession is made unto salvation.*

After you have accepted Christ as Lord and Savior for the forgiveness of your sins, you become a child of God. Your next step is to be baptized, learn the Bible, and be discipled. Pray for God to send a spiritually mature person to disciple you. If you prayed the above prayer for the first time after reading this book, it is my pleasure to welcome you to God's family. Kindly drop me a note to inform me of your decision at TheHappinessCode@yahoo.com

Works Cited

- Matthew Henry's Complete Commentary on the Bible

- John Gill's Exposition on the Whole Bible

- Jamieson, Fausset, and Brown's Commentary on the Whole Bible

About the Author

I grew up in a small fishing village in northern Malaysia, bordering Thailand. My family practiced Taoism in a Muslim country. We worshiped idols and ancestors. My dad maintained three altars at home—for the god of wealth, the god of the earth, and ancestors. He offered a daily drink offering of tea, oil for the lamps, and incense in the morning and evening. He asked the gods and ancestors for protection and blessings. On festival days he set out meat offerings of chicken or duck and sweet cakes, which ended up as our dinner.

We went to temples on special occasions, such as for fortune-telling, to celebrate the birthdays of our favorite gods, to get the best dates for travel, weddings, building, moving, or starting a new business, and to ask for healing and financial blessings, normally in the form of lottery numbers. Indeed, everyone that I knew asked for three common things—wealth, health, and more wealth. No one ever kneeled down to an idol and said, "Forgive me, I am a sinner."

I was sick a lot in my early years. Grandma frequently took me to the temple, which was only about 100 yards away. At one point the priest decided that I should be adopted by the god of heaven. And so I was given to him. That meant I had to appear before the god of heaven once a year with offerings and thanksgiving. I can't remember if my sickness went away, but obviously I survived. When I was 15, my grandma decided I needed to be redeemed from the god of heaven, otherwise I would not prosper. It didn't mean anything to me, but I did what I was told. I went to the temple with incense and offerings and thanked the god of heaven for his protection and told him that I didn't need him anymore.

Our concept of gods and ghosts was simple. We believed them and didn't want to offend them. They could be for us or against us, so we worshiped and bribed them for our personal benefit.

Hell was real. Asians who practice Taoism know that they will die and go to hell. This knowledge was passed down to me by my grandparents in my early years. When Christians in the U.S. told me that I was going to split hell wide open, this was no new revelation.

I was taught that the hell god will judge the dead according to their works. Those with excellent good works will cross the chasm on the golden bridge without punishment and be reincarnated as privileged humans. Those with good works that outweigh their bad works use the silver bridge without punishment, but will be reincarnated as humans with fewer privileges. Those who were bad will be severely punished and tortured in hell.

However, I was taught that punishments could be reduced if living relatives burned hell money, houses, cars, and maids made of bamboo and paper as offerings to the hell god. I watched my dad burn those things to the hell god soon after my grandpa died. He burned stacks of hell notes, which came in extremely large denominations, as much as $2 billion apiece. The total amount had to be in the gazillions. I thought to myself that things must be very expensive down there. At the end of the burning, a small twister wind came and picked up the ashes. I was freaked out, but was comforted when my dad told me that the hell god had received the offerings.

I was further taught that the Wheel of Reincarnation and the Pavilion of Forgetfulness are in the Tenth Court of hell. After serving their sentences, sinners arrive at the Tenth Court to receive their final judgment from the hell god. Thereafter they are brought to the Pavilion of Forgetfulness, where an old lady, Meng Po, hands them a cup of magic tea, which makes them forget their past lives. They then go through the Wheel of Reincarnation where some are reborn as humans and some as animals, depending on their past deeds. Some are reborn into a life of ease and comfort, while others into sorrow and suffering.

Life in a small fishing village was good, slow, and peaceful. People knew each other and dropped by for a visit without an appointment. My family didn't have much. I spent a lot of time at my neighbor's house watching black and white TV. It was a piece of furniture with a small tube. I grew up watching Wild, Wild West, Gun Smoke, Bonanza, The Andy Griffith Show, Looney Tunes, and Disney programs. I love Bugs Bunny to this day.

Behind the closed doors of most Chinese families, parents put intense pressure on their children to succeed. My parents always compared me to other kids. When I did not achieve at school, I would hear them say, "You lousy...," "You stupid...," "You useless..." It was their way of challenging, motivating, and preparing me for the real world. Most Chinese parents in their generation adopted this motivation method. Today I thank them, because they toughened me for the competition on a global platform. The intense pressure was driven by two main reasons. 1) The official retirement age is 55. Males particularly have to succeed by age 30, so the ramp up is short and steep. There is no time to party. 2) The Chinese society is very materialistic. People are judged by their possessions. A Chinese male who does not own a house, a Mercedes Benz, and a Rolex watch by age 30 is considered an underachiever. (Bear in mind, those things cost several times more over there than in the U.S.) The guys who don't get rich by age 30 have a tough time getting a date. So life to me was about money, fast money, and lots of money, by hook or by crook, and I joined the materialistic society.

I was transferred to Kuala Lumpur, the capital of Malaysia, in my freshman year for higher education. The move was like dropping someone who couldn't swim into an ocean with no floatation. I went from the serene and beautiful beaches of the South China Sea to a rat-race, glitzy concrete jungle. I had to learn so many new things, almost all at once. I was so handicapped compared to the city kids. My attire, mannerisms, and speech betrayed me. Things like disco and break dancing while holding a stereo the size of small luggage was so foreign to me. Thankfully I was able to make rapid changes and excelled in school. Unfortunately I was also exposed to the five vices of happiness—eating, drinking, womanizing, gambling, and smoking. That was the definition of a successful and happy man.

While I was in college, my parents decided to send all my siblings to Kuala Lumpur for education and bought a house for us to live in. My sister attended the St. Mary girls' school and was the first to become a Christian in my family. Soon after, my parents retired and moved in. The next thing I knew, mom was reading the Bible. That infuriated me. Christianity divided my family—the ladies were Christians, the boys were Taoists. From then on I hated the Christian religion and my Christian friends. I treated them badly.

I was one of the earliest computer science graduates in Malaysia. I had a computer job before I graduated and worked in the industry for a few years. Computers, especially personal computers, were so new at the time. It took two men to carry an 80 MB hard drive. I wish I kept the Apple II and the Mac. I still have a stack of punch cards and a stack of hard drives the size of a large pizza to remind me of the good old days.

I was increasingly dissatisfied with the open discrimination by the Malaysian government against the Chinese and Indians, and decided to move abroad. I was choosing between Australia and the U.S. Since I grew up watching American TV programs, I chose and came to the U.S. in 1990 with the hope of seeing cowboys in person and making lots of dollars so I could return to Malaysia to live like a king.

Life in the U.S. was a reboot and tough in the beginning. Yet again I found myself having to assimilate into a foreign culture. I ended up in Kansas City and fell in love with the place and the people. The Midwesterners were so friendly and helpful.

One day a coworker invited me to church. I reluctantly agreed, because she was my supervisor. I can't remember what was said during the service, but I went forward to the altar during the invitation. Pastor Gary Staab greeted me and offered to teach me the Bible. We met each Saturday morning at his house for about a year. He taught me the basic doctrines and principles from the Bible. I realized the significance of my sins for the very first time. (I previously thought sin was no big deal because the hell god could be bribed, and there was reincarnation.) I learned the truth that sin condemned me to death, and all my good works were unable to cleanse me or purchase the required redemption. I was separated from God. I looked for a solution in my old religion, but none of the idols, monks, and priests could give me eternal life. I discovered eternal life was a gift from God through Jesus Christ. In 1994, by faith I accepted Jesus Christ as my Lord and Savior for the pardoning of my sins.

God is sovereign. A Taoist kid from a little-known small fishing village set off in search of worldly success and happiness, but by the grace of God, found eternal life, true riches, peace, and purpose. I am forever in debt to and thankful for the Lord Jesus Christ. I am also thankful for the faithful people whom God put in my life to teach and guide me in His truth.

I am now serving the Lord in the juvenile detention ministry, Friends of International Students ministry, and am partnering with native pastors in India and Nepal. Feel free to email me with your comments and suggestions at TheHappinessCode@yahoo.com.

The Will of the Enemy

Jody Shee

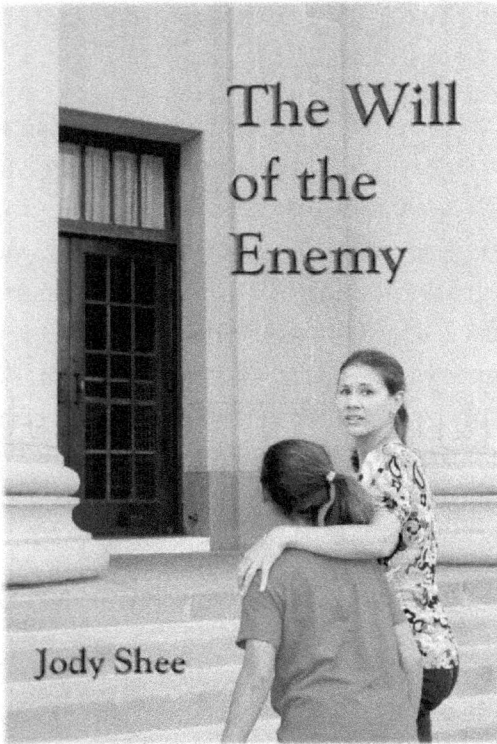

An inspirational suspense novel from Purple Dreamer Publishers available on Amazon

In 1987, Julie Bradley kidnaps her daughter, stunning everyone who knows her. She has no other alternative to keep her abusive ex-husband from getting at their daughter. Julie's policeman ex-father-in-law wants his granddaughter back, in spite of the horrific things his son has done to her. Like bloodhounds, law enforcement is always one heart-pounding step behind them. For how long can they escape? Will Julie's primitive motherly instincts be enough to match the will of the enemy? Three things keep Julie grounded: her journal, a Psalm, and her daughter. One thing is certain, they will never live ordinary lives.

Jody Shee

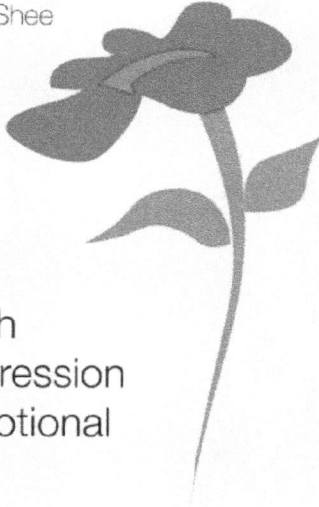

Ditch
Depression
Devotional

*31 Days to Biblical Hope, Peace
and Emotional Balance*

A 31-day
devotional
guide to
biblical hope,
peace and
emotional
balance
available on
Amazon

Depression does not take God by surprise. What seems like a crisis to us is an opportunity to Him. Relief starts with an understanding of His viewpoint. This 31-day devotional looks at the topic of depression four ways: Common causes; depression's spiritual benefits (there are some!); God's loving rescue; and Bible character overcomers. This book is especially useful to new believers, singles and moms. Besides a short daily reading, it includes: Daily "going deeper" sections for those who want to explore the topic further; a life-altering assignment to complete by the end of the book; links to helpful songs; and online free frameable verse pictures. While it is meant for personal use to complete in one month, it is also appropriate for use in a classroom or small-group setting with a free online leader's guide available on mastertruth.com.

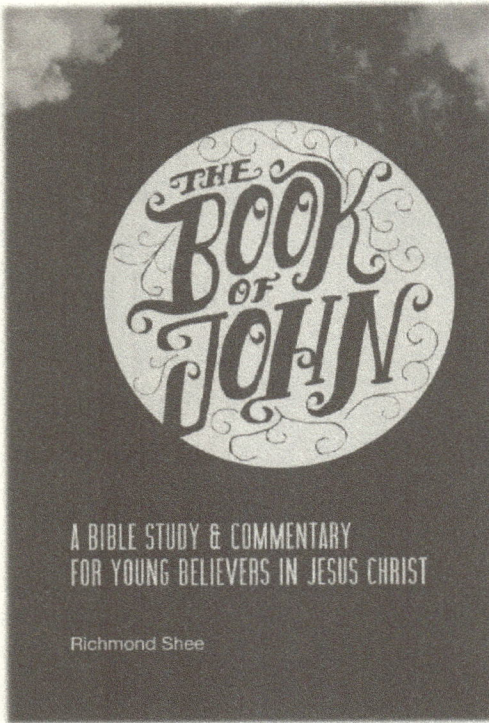

THE BOOK OF JOHN

A BIBLE STUDY & COMMENTARY
FOR YOUNG BELIEVERS IN JESUS CHRIST

Richmond Shee

"Read the Gospel of John," is the advice often given to young believers in Jesus Christ. Richmond Shee, a former Buddhist, received the same advice many years ago. In this book, he sets out to show the rich, three-dimensional nature of the Gospel of John, covering the historical, inspirational, and prophetic angles in each chapter, which are frequently revealed in pictures, types, and numbers. He includes illustrations throughout to summarize truth in a simple, inviting way--something visual learners do not have with other commentaries. The book is also filled with verse cross-references, allowing the reader to dig deeper on any topic at any time. The layout of each chapter serves as an example to the reader of how to systematically outline and study a book of the Bible. Get ready for a lively look at the Gospel of John.